Inspiring, informative, an[...] everyone raising a busy family. Kathryn shares her personal journey as a military spouse and provides powerful pearls of wisdom (a.k.a., "triumphant thinking") that will help you achieve incredible success. In a candid and transparent manner, she speaks about marriage, relationships, child-raising, dealing with the vicissitudes of life, and coping with unfulfilled goals. You will cheer, cry, and gasp as you read her story. What a blessing and gift to military (and nonmilitary) families. It is much more than a memoir. It is a guide that will help you overcome challenges and be triumphant as you write your own story. Hooah!

—Dr. Preston Butler, LTC, U.S. Army, Retired

Triumphant in the Trenches is a story that can only be told by someone who has lived through the many perils of life as a military spouse. This story, about overcoming, championing, rising, and succeeding after thirty-five years of service as a counselor and mentor, is indeed noteworthy. Kathryn's memoirs of a military spouse are compelling. She comes straight from the heart as she shares her gripping stories written with transparency, sensitivity, and grace. They will stay with the readers long after the final page is turned. She masterfully weaves through the issues of military life. Her strong faith and exceptional insight give us a vivid description into a story of hope and determination Kathryn's experiences evoke. This is a must-read for women from all walks of life.

—Dr. Barbara McCoo Lewis, General Supervisor, International Department of Women, COGIC; Jurisdictional Supervisor, Southern California First Ecclesiastical Jurisdiction

Kathryn Butler is a military spouse with over thirty years of experience in the military community, working as a mentor, career coach, family readiness trainer, and public speaker. Through her personal journey, you will discover impactful anecdotes, insight, and inspiring tips. This seasoned military spouse shares with the reader her personal struggles as a wife working to save her marriage, as a mother setting a solid foundation for her children, and as a career professional in search of her identity—dealing with the loss of family and friends and finding strength through her faith. This book is long overdue! It is a treasure chest, overflowing with sage advice for military spouses of all ages.

—Derrick Christovale Sr. SgtMaj, USMC, Retired

Inspirational, transparent, and genuine honesty—the words on the pages of this book of memoirs speaks volumes to the life and legacy of a true overcomer. Kathryn's positive outlook on the trials and tribulations of life are very uplifting and insightful. This book is the perfect combination of inspirational stories, life's lessons, anecdotes to the trials and tribulations of life.

Every military spouse needs to have a Kathryn Butler in their life—someone to give you truth and wisdom. This is a book that is inspirational, uplifting, and authentic and will help get you through the highs and lows of life.

—Mattrice Williamson, military spouse, wife, and mother

Triumphant in the Trenches is a must-read that you will return to again and again. Kathryn's authentic and inspiring life lessons, triumphant thinking tips, and "mind-itudes" create an empowering roadmap to victory. She helps us understand how investing in ourselves allows our inner warrior to rise! As Kathryn says, "We have the power to change our environment and impact the lives we touch each day if we stay true to who we are." Thank you, Kathryn, for your dedication to true servant leadership, your lifelong service to our military community, and your inspiration to all of us to live each season triumphantly.

—Lana Massimini, disabled Vietnam veteran's spouse, certified career coach

Triumphant in the Trenches is the written expression of Kathryn Butler's love and passion for military spouses. Kathryn masterfully and skillfully shares her life story to help military spouses overcome their personal life challenges. This is a must-read for both military and civilian spouses alike. You'll be not only touched and inspired but also empowered to make choices that result in successful living.

—Pastor Michael N. Henderson, Gospel Light Church, Santa Ana, California

TRIUMPHANT IN THE TRENCHES
(VICTORY DESPITE CHALLENGES)

Memoirs of a Military Spouse

KATHRYN A. BUTLER

WESTBOW PRESS®
A DIVISION OF THOMAS NELSON & ZONDERVAN

Copyright © 2020 Kathryn A. Butler.

All rights reserved. No part of this book may be used or reproduced by any means, graphic, electronic, or mechanical, including photocopying, recording, taping or by any information storage retrieval system without the written permission of the author except in the case of brief quotations embodied in critical articles and reviews.

This book is a work of non-fiction. Unless otherwise noted, the author and the publisher make no explicit guarantees as to the accuracy of the information contained in this book and in some cases, names of people and places have been altered to protect their privacy.

WestBow Press books may be ordered through booksellers or by contacting:

WestBow Press
A Division of Thomas Nelson & Zondervan
1663 Liberty Drive
Bloomington, IN 47403
www.westbowpress.com
1 (866) 928-1240

Because of the dynamic nature of the Internet, any web addresses or links contained in this book may have changed since publication and may no longer be valid. The views expressed in this work are solely those of the author and do not necessarily reflect the views of the publisher, and the publisher hereby disclaims any responsibility for them.

Any people depicted in stock imagery provided by Getty Images are models, and such images are being used for illustrative purposes only. Certain stock imagery © Getty Images.

Cover art designed by Beau Kimbrel

ISBN: 978-1-9736-9339-0 (sc)
ISBN: 978-1-9736-9338-3 (hc)
ISBN: 978-1-9736-9340-6 (e)

Library of Congress Control Number: 2020910116

Print information available on the last page.

WestBow Press rev. date: 08/18/2020

Dedication

To all who have experienced the challenges and triumphs of life, whether military or civilian. To everyone who has sacrificed their dreams and aspirations to enhance, uplift, and impact the life of another. To those who have felt abandoned, isolated, or misplaced as they have navigated the journey of life. To each of you, I salute you and hope that you find some sense of recognition in these pages that will bring a smile and sense of acknowledgment to your existence. To my deceased parents, Bishop Fred D. Lawson, Jr. (WWII Army veteran) and Mrs. Erma June Anderson Lawson; my deceased siblings, Kay Lawson Roseman (Vietnam Navy veteran), Fred D. Lawson III, and James O. Lawson I (Vietnam Marine Corps veteran). You are gone but never forgotten.

CONTENTS

Acknowledgments xi
Foreword xiii
Preface xv

SECTION 1: TRAINING GROUND

Chapter 1   Backstory 1
Chapter 2   In the Beginning 5
Chapter 3   Boot Camp 10
Chapter 4   First Duty Station 14

SECTION 2: ENDURING THE STRUGGLE

Chapter 5   Battleground 21
Chapter 6   Right Place – Wrong People 27
Chapter 7   Advance or Retreat—It's Your Choice 33
Chapter 8   The Test 38

SECTION 3: GROWTH TACTICS

Chapter 9   The Impact of Loss 47
Chapter 10   The Unexpected Gift 52
Chapter 11   A Life-Changing Experience 58
Chapter 12   Test for the Next Level (Northern Virginia) 62

SECTION 4: SUCCESS INITIATIVES

Chapter 13   Volunteering—It Makes a Difference (South Korea) 71
Chapter 14   Be Teachable 77

Chapter 15 Invest in the Future 82
Chapter 16 The Shift 88

SECTION 5: STRATEGIC ALIGNMENT

Chapter 17 Networking.. 99
Chapter 18 Leadership vs. Servanthood 104
Chapter 19 The Next Game Plan...113
Chapter 20 Delayed but Not Denied 119
Chapter 21 Sacrifice—That's What We Do 124

Conclusion - BIG! BIG! BIG! 131
Triumphant Thinking (Nuggets of Wisdom) 135
References 139
About the Author 141
Author's Note 143

ACKNOWLEDGMENTS

I want to acknowledge my amazing husband, Dr. Preston Butler, Jr., who is my champion and the love of my life. Thank you for your undeniable belief in me. Your constant support and push enabled me to complete this project. Thank you for the opportunity to travel the world, to experience life at its best, and to chase my dreams, which are overtaking me now. I am forever humbled and grateful for you.

To my phenomenal children and their spouses, Chelsi Butler Alabi (John), Preston Butler III (Christine), and my "mini-me," Celeste, I love each of you unconditionally and thank you for living "on purpose" to be the best, most authentic human beings you can be. I appreciate your inputs, insights, and encouragement during the last two years, while I focused my energy on this project. May your lives be forever enriched because of it.

To my spiritual influencers and counselors—Mother Barbara McCoo Lewis, International Supervisor of Women, COGIC; and Mother Romanetha Stallworth, Supervisor of Women, Kentucky, First Jurisdiction, COGIC—I am forever humbled by your prayers and immeasurable faith in me to complete this assignment.

To each of the wonderful, professional, and insightful friends who read and revised the manuscript and offered suggestions to make it better, thank you for your precious time and commitment to help me accomplish a long-awaited dream. I pray that you will be rewarded greatly for your labor of love.

FOREWORD

Triumphant in the Trenches is a breath of fresh air in an increasingly situational, excuse-ridden world of family challenges, especially the brave men and women who serve in our military. Kathryn Butler manages to combine compassion with her highly motivated, put-your-best-foot-forward thinking, offering a balanced how-to narrative for spouses to overcome the vicissitudes of military life.

Kathy offers a keen awareness of how ideas, practices, and life responsibilities take on new meaning and how a shift in our thought processes can produce new outcomes. Here you'll find no superficial platitudes that gloss over or minimize the imbalances of military life (tours of duty and home life). Rather, you'll find an insightful (yet typically avoided) discussion on how "triumphant thinking" can yield victory despite the trenches, all the way through military separation or retirement.

Kathy's integration of the seven stages of the emotional cycle of deployment highly influences her triumphant thinking in the trenches of her own life and that of her family.

This book is a must-read, whether you are military or civilian.

—Romanetha Stallworth, M.Ed., Marriage & Family Therapist

PREFACE

On a Tuesday afternoon, while I was assisting one of my students preparing for transition out of the military, a marine staff sergeant stepped into the office space that I shared with three other colleagues and stood quietly with a blank stare on his face. The space was cramped. We each had a cubicle area with a desk and two chairs so that we could manage the necessary paperwork and provide guidance and resources to the fifty or more students assigned to each of us for the one-week Transition Readiness Class.

This day, I sat in the first cubicle as you entered the office. I was assisting a student while two of my colleagues were in the two cubicles behind me, discussing various work-related challenges. Because I was the first to see the gentleman, I excused myself from the conversation with my student and inquired if there was anything I could help him with.

For some reason, the gentleman made eye contact with one of my colleagues, but he spoke to me and said, "I need assistance with paperwork to get out." It was interesting. The gentleman never acknowledged that I had asked if I could assist him; he just moved into our cubicle space, his eyes locked on my colleague behind me to the right. During the conversation between my two colleagues, there was an exchange of laughter that was somehow taken in offense by the staff sergeant. Suddenly, the gentleman moved in toward me, flailing his arms and yelling, "Stand down ... stand down!"

My reaction was to stand up in front of him, ask him to stand down, and leave the office until he could take a breath and calm down. By this time, my other two colleagues had stood up and realized this was a hostile situation.

I asked the gentleman to reenter and calmly state what he needed. He then continued to say that I was laughing at him and owed him an apology. The colleague with whom he had previously locked eyes stepped up to say he would help him and took him into the hallway. I finished assisting my student, who was also shaken and wondering why the gentleman had reacted the way he did. A few minutes later, my colleague returned with the gentleman and escorted him into the back office to talk to another colleague. After about ten minutes, they came out, and before the gentleman departed the office, he turned to me and said, "You owe me an apology." I informed him that I was not the one laughing and that it was simply a misunderstanding. He left yelling and saying over and over, "You owe me an apology."

This was the first time in over twenty years of working with military service and family members that I felt threatened. Yes, I had experienced PTSD (post-traumatic stress disorder). I couldn't sleep for the next few days and was jumpy every time someone entered the office. I called the military police to file a report because I felt my surroundings were not safe, and I was not sure of this individual's intent.

After thinking it all through and rehearsing the steps in my mind, I realized I had been taught to deal with people in threatening situations, that I was in control, and that I would not allow my fear or this person's actions to paralyze me. This made me think about the many spouses who work or volunteer on the hundreds of installations and how we develop resiliency and the power to adapt instantly to critical situations. The fact that I survived yet another triumph in the trenches prompted me to tell my story.

So why write a book about the life of a military spouse and how I navigated through this lifestyle? After thirty-five years of moving, counseling, mentoring, adjusting, redefining, adapting, sacrificing, suffering, overcoming, championing, rising, and succeeding, I felt it necessary to put pen to paper to offer validation to the many spouses who have also survived. I also wanted to provide a realistic viewpoint and insights that will bring hope to the many spouses currently living the life and to those whose journey is to come.

For sure, many stories have been shared—from other military spouses and those married to A-type personalities to CEOs, public figures, professional athletes, actors, preachers, and many more. So many have lived in a "glass bowl," having to navigate the limelight, the ridicule, the lack of privacy, the sacrificing of family time, and even their careers. I want to share my story in the hope that even one individual reading it—who may be feeling hopeless, forgotten, pushed aside, misunderstood, and not validated—will know that they too can be *triumphant in the trenches*.

SECTION 1

Training Ground

We are all too familiar with tests as we begin taking them early in life at school, but you wil l discover in the next four chapters: (1) "Backstory," (2) "In the Beginning," (3) "Boot Camp," and (4) "First Duty Station"—that your commitment to keeping a marriage and sustaining your identity are tests that many will struggle to pass.

CHAPTER 1

Backstory

Let's begin. I grew up in Stillwater, Oklahoma, a small town with the beautiful Oklahoma State University at its center. I was raised by a Pentecostal pastor and a kind, gentle, and wise mother who set me on a course to become the woman I am today. Little did I know the path my life would take and the exposure to the plethora of opportunities, cultures, countries, and experiences I would have that would shape my life.

Being the youngest of six children afforded me the luxury of being spoiled, even though my family lived below the poverty line, of which I was totally unaware. Wearing clothing from yard sales, secondhand stores, and hand-me-downs was normal for me. Amazingly, my clothes were always clean, pressed, and fancy, with added ribbons and bows to enhance the washed-out previously-owned item.

I was a feisty little girl, and since I was allowed to express my ideas, joys, and dreams, I was full of love, laughter, and optimism. Mind you, this was during the 1960s, a tumultuous time in our country when we were beset by many social and political issues. However, I was oblivious to this, as my family sheltered me and encouraged me to be myself and live without limits and inhibitions.

When each of my siblings finished high school, they left home, one by one. I really never thought too much of it, but I knew the strong hand of my father and his very strict house rules were probably the primary reasons they left. I realized that the freedoms I was afforded developed a strong personality and voice in me, and that voice wanted to be heard.

During my senior year of high school, I had the awesome opportunity to travel to Europe with the Oklahoma Chorale to sing in five different countries. This gave me a new sense of adventure and appreciation for culture. It also gave me a false sense of myself. I felt as if I was ready to tackle the world and no one was going to impede my progress.

After a few nights of disobeying my curfew, my father and I concluded that for us to have any decent relationship, I would need to move out on my own. It was a tough time and definitely a learning experience. Fortunately, my supervisor at work offered me to stay with her and her husband until they moved into a bigger space.

This is where my journey began, and admittedly, I made many mistakes that could have destroyed my life. Poor choices threw me into the trenches. I think it is fairly common that children who come from homes with strict guidelines, boundaries, and high moral standards at some point find themselves rebelling, trying to find their own identity. I think rebellion is common in the lives of most teenagers. That is exactly where I found myself, and to be honest, it was truly only the grace of God that kept me from becoming my own worst nightmare.

My late-teen years were marked by riotous living, keeping dangerous company, and experimenting with whatever my friends suggested. I woke up one morning feeling desperate, sick, and tired of being sick and tired. I realized I had allowed others to influence the direction my life was taking. It was on a downward spiral. I knew I had much to look forward to and that this lifestyle was not going to get me there. So I took a courageous stand and faced my mistakes. I chose not to allow guilt to ruin me, and I chose to rise out of the trenches.

I want to take you on my journey. It's my story, and it is intended to shed light on the life of a woman who has experienced great joys, disappointments, and victories throughout the last thirty years or so—all built on phenomenal life experiences in the military. My story may not reflect the lives of others, but as I have had the opportunity to share, comfort, and lift up thousands of spouses over the years, I have written it for the one who is feeling lost, hopeless, and forgotten. You too can be triumphant in the trenches.

Throughout my academic years, from first grade to college, I strove to bridge gaps between races, cultures, social statuses, and people in general. There were events in my life that made me realize there is so much more to life than I had experienced so far—and that I could have it all.

My mother worked as a domestic engineer (housekeeper/nanny/cook) for the president of Oklahoma State University and would often take me to work with her. While she was the housekeeper for one wonderful family, each time the children of that family were enrolled in a class, lesson, or opportunity, so was I. Equestrian classes, swimming lessons, dirt bikes, and travel were all provided for me as if I was part of the family.

Being exposed to proper etiquette and protocols at an early age prepared me for my future as the wife of a military officer and mother of three phenomenal children. It also enhanced my ability to mentor and to be an effective role model to a host of men and women across the United States and abroad.

I grew up singing in the church choir and playing the trumpet from grade six through college. This, as well as being an actress, opened my mind to different views and let me mingle with people from different backgrounds and cultures. The discipline I gained as a performer taught me that to attain greatness, one needs to stay focused and apply oneself at every level.

I performed in my high school theater productions and select chorus groups, and as I mentioned earlier, in my senior year, I toured Europe along with the Oklahoma Chorale. In preparation for this tour, we spent many hours in rehearsals, constantly going over our parts. We would represent not only the state of Oklahoma but the United States as a whole. We visited Germany, Switzerland, France, Belgium, and Holland. Flying across the country with classmates was a huge step to take, and it was the first time I traveled as a young adult on my own. This opportunity created a passion for traveling abroad and learning other languages—adding to my desire to connect with all people and to bridge any gaps I encountered.

I always had an interest in meeting different people and getting to know them, their culture, beliefs, and upbringing. It didn't matter who I was with or where I was; I always had a positive experience meeting others, and I always walked away as a better person.

I must say, although my life has been tremendously blessed, it has not been without challenges and struggles. But I wouldn't change a thing, because my experiences molded me and defined who I am today.

For this book, to be *triumphant* means to win, to be victorious, to overcome an obstacle, or achieve success. According to the dictionary, a *trench* is a long, narrow ditch. I use the word trench metaphorically throughout the book to refer to a challenge, struggle, or obstacle. Therefore, the title of this book, *Triumphant in the Trenches*, declares that one can be victorious while crawling through a ditch, while going through a conflict, warfare, or difficult time, or even while fighting for one's survival.

CHAPTER 2

In the Beginning

After graduating from high school in 1978, I matriculated into Oklahoma State University (OSU). Yes, I went to high school and college in the same town, which was okay, because OSU was a great Big 8 (now Big 12) university. I was a member of the marching band, the jazz band, and the music sorority, Tau Beta Sigma. I worked part-time in retail at a ladies' clothing store, and I had my own apartment and car. I was cruising through college and enjoying the ride as an independent woman.

During the first three years of college, I was in and out of a few relationships that didn't have any substance. I felt as if I needed to focus on finishing school since I hadn't committed to doing as well as I should have. I also didn't want to disappoint my parents, who had sacrificed much for me to attend.

Then, at the start of my junior year, my life changed dramatically. I met the love of my life and began the journey that would allow me to accomplish and experience some of my wildest dreams and aspirations. My soon-to-be husband had just completed two years of schooling at New Mexico Military Institute and transferred to OSU to complete his bachelor's degree. He had received a commission as a second lieutenant in the United States Army Reserve, and the plan for his life was already in motion.

My first challenge as his fiancée was dealing with another woman whose friends had convinced her that my husband was going to marry her. She was persistent. This was an interesting turn of events, and there were a few heated discussions, but she finally came to her senses and realized we were going to be married and she was not going to be in the picture. We married at the beginning of our senior year in college. Trust me, this was not the only time another woman had her sights on my husband, but none would prevail. We made a commitment and took an oath to love, cherish, and honor each other, through the good and the bad, and to be loyal and supportive as we began this life long journey into the unknown.

I didn't realize the gravity and impact it would have on me. It would take me away from my home, my family, and my small-town place of security. Not only had my husband signed up to serve in the military, but as a spouse, I had joined as well, figuratively speaking. We were one and, therefore, thrown into the trenches of life together.

No one prepared me for this private world filled with a million and one acronyms and protocols. I didn't have a mentor that scooped me up and helped me to navigate the do's and don'ts—how to dress and when to stand and when to sit. I came in as naive as they come and just my friendly, open-to-everyone self. I had not dealt with any real diversity issues or status challenges, but now, suddenly, I was thrown into the fight and had to figure it out. Although uncomfortable sometimes, I was determined not to allow others' insecurities and inadequacies to change my character.

Not everyone celebrates your victories or accomplishments, especially when they may come at the cost of someone else not receiving it. My husband was a go-getter, a hard worker, and a man of integrity. He didn't compete with others but set the standard bar very high for himself. He was getting promoted ahead of schedule and was selected to command as the youngest commander at the installation at our first duty station. There were plenty of haters, but they didn't deter him from accomplishing his task.

This type of drive doesn't just happen. From the young age of nine, he started his first business, cutting yards. He did pretty well for himself and began a lifelong journey as a businessman while on active duty. We ventured into several businesses along the way. He was very disciplined and I would say somewhat of a tightwad when it came to money, and I was the opposite; I was the youngest in my family, and I pretty much got what I wanted. This adjustment in our personalities was a true test and was one of the many differences we discovered.

There I was, fresh out of college, still a newlywed and trying to figure out how to be a wife and still have my own identity in a new environment. This is a common situation in marriage. It takes maturity and time to grow together and function as a unit while still maintaining your self-identity, self-worth, and value. This was my lifelong commitment to myself.

I wasn't working when we moved to our first duty station, and my days were filled with the mundane since we didn't have any children and I didn't know many people outside my in-laws who just happened to live in the same town. This new space I was occupying pushed my emotional state to a place of second-guessing whether this was the lifestyle for me.

I was a jovial, outgoing person who loved to meet new people and share my passions and talents in any way I could. But not everyone was as welcoming and willing to move past their personal baggage and upbringing, which were noticeably different from mine.

About a year or so after arriving at our first duty station, I landed a job as a weekend reporter and assistant morning producer at the local TV station, KSWO 7News. My degree in broadcast journalism was finally paying off, and I felt validated and energized that I could move forward into my destiny. You would have thought this was a time of joy and excitement in our marriage, but actually, it pushed us further apart.

Little did I know that my husband was considering a divorce. Yes, the big D-word. Some years later, I found this out while collaborating on our first book together. I was shocked, to say the least. In our early days as a young military couple, we experienced some of the same challenges couples are facing today: poor or no communication, feelings of abandonment, misunderstanding, mistrust, and isolation. I didn't understand that these were the things I was feeling or dealing with because I had never been in this place before. How did I overcome and work my way through it? It all began with a change in mindset.

Once my husband made up in his mind that he would fight for our marriage and make some changes in how he viewed it—mainly, taking the responsibility himself—I followed his lead. As he changed and shifted his way of communicating, so did I.

This was not easy, and it took both of us to willingly put our issues aside to listen to what the other was saying and needed. Did we fail sometimes? Sure, but that's what kept us moving forward. With each failure came a time of growth, trust, and forgiveness. This was the first trench and triumph we experienced as a couple.

Triumphant Thinking

1. Great relationships are the result of the investment. Plan to commit your time and energy for the long haul.
2. Revisit expectations often, they change just as you will.
3. Learn the art of effective communication and use it.

CHAPTER 3

Boot Camp

Attending boot camp is the first training that prepares you for the missions ahead. So what exactly does boot camp entail? I have never been to boot camp, but based on what I've heard from many that have gone through it, the experience, especially when referring to a military boot camp, is designed to make or break you. It is a series of rigorous training events designed to shape your thinking process and test your physical and mental ability as a means to set you up for success in future assignments.

My husband attended the Reserved Officers' Training Corps (ROTC) basic and advanced boot camps as part of the army's early commissioning program through New Mexico Military Institute. He was commissioned a second lieutenant after completing the two-year program and joined the Oklahoma National Guard. By the time he completed his bachelor's degree at OSU, he was promoted to first lieutenant.

The first year of marriage was a joy, and although we were busy with school and work, we seemed to be adjusting to our new life together and looking forward with great anticipation to our future. But now the make-or-break-you concept was introduced to us, as our lives began to take shape in different ways, and we were tested on how we would blend our very different personalities. Compromise and sometimes disappointment were the key components in our development at this point.

I had a very thriving life, as I had just completed my reign as a college queen and had the pleasure of building vital relationships with other contestants from various backgrounds and ethnicities. We worked hard to bridge gaps on our college campus and created an atmosphere of respect and mutuality of ideas and beliefs. I loved music and performing with the college marching band and jazz band, as well as acting in the local community theater.

As a broadcast journalism major with an emphasis in mass communication, I planned to follow in the footsteps of Oprah Winfrey and become the next big talk show host. Needless to say, I was very busy and fairly popular in the arenas that I was circulating, and I thought my plan was sure to take flight as soon as I graduated from college. Little did I know, the true "boot camp" was about to commence.

Now I am embarking upon a new journey with an individual who had committed his life to a military lifestyle as a tenth grader in high school where he participated in Junior ROTC and graduated as a cadet colonel and battalion commander. The differences in mindsets still were not drastic yet because we were both raised in a very strict Pentecostal religious home with high moral standards and regulations that gave us a common foundation. But I was now married to a military officer whose career was basically set in motion before we met, and now my choices were about to be challenged. This was not the direction I had planned for my life, but it was the one I was in, and I had to make a choice: go with it or get out of it.

The test of mental and emotional stability had now begun. The expectations that were now before us were quite different and not quite what we thought they would be. Our own relationship "boot camp" was about to begin.

We were raised in Oklahoma and had similar family backgrounds. Both fathers were pastors within the same denomination. Both families had six children and placed a high emphasis on education, and yet we were very different. I was a free spirit and was engaged with everyone and just about everything. My husband was not thrilled with the idea of sharing me with the world because it detracted from our time together.

Changes that were taking place were causing me to adjust my personality. What I didn't realize is that when you love someone and want to please them, you may find yourself going along with what they want for the sake of peace. This happens with both parties in the relationship, and while this is neither right nor wrong, it does need to be addressed. This could develop into a problem where an individual starts to lose his/her identity and could become resentful.

Since I am a peacekeeper, I made it work positively by allowing myself to grow and mature within our relationship. It is not an easy process. It takes commitment and patience for this to work. Some days, I would ask myself if this was more than I could handle, but the other choices would have deterred me from my destiny. In retrospect, I just didn't understand at that time that the plan for my life was already set in motion.

Marriage is wonderful, but it requires a lifetime of selflessness.

We didn't solicit any marriage counseling or guidance on how to blend our finances or to set joint goals before we were married, and because our parents had both been married for over forty years at this time, we felt we knew what to expect and that love was pretty much all we needed. We realized the hard way that we were wrong. Expectations were something that we hadn't discussed, and they were definitely not being met as we had planned. Now I realized the importance of counseling and the positive impact it would have made if we received it before making one of the biggest decisions in our lives. *Marriage is wonderful, but it requires a lifetime of selflessness.*

This is a very important conversation that needs to take place before marriage. Often, we have unrealistic expectations because we have witnessed unrealistic role models. We may have gained them from watching the fantasy of relationships on television where the lives of the rich and famous portray no problems, the perfect house with the white picket fence and perfect family. We may have based our perceptions on our own family life, be it imperfect, single-parent, or other circumstances that gave us a misconception of what a marriage looks like. It was a reality check.

Triumphant Thinking

1. You need to know what you're getting yourself into before you marry, there will be an adjustment phase. Seek counsel or guidance before and after marriage.
2. Discuss your family principles and values to gain a better understanding of who he or she is.
3. Realize that your validation does not come only from your spouse. You must know who you are and the value you bring to the relationship.

CHAPTER 4

First Duty Station

Can you believe it? Both born and raised in Oklahoma, and now we were joining the military to see the world, and our first duty station was Fort Sill, Oklahoma. You couldn't have paid me to believe this is where we would spend our first four years of active duty.

We literally moved from my hometown to my husband's hometown. At first, this seemed like a great idea; we would be close enough to make trips to visit my mother and father whenever I wanted, and we'd have time with my husband's family as well. It was great, but it came with an unexpected set of adjustments.

Remember, I am married to a high achiever who has always wanted to be in the military and certainly wanted to excel in his career—and excel he did, at everything he put his mind to. The first opportunity for that trait to shine came during our first tour of duty. Things were looking great when he reported to his company commander. However, it was a much different story when he reported to his battalion commander. My husband expected a warm welcome but received just the opposite.

When he reported to the battalion commander for his initial meeting, rather than being greeted with the words "Welcome to the battalion," he was greeted with the words, "I saw your bio and was glad to see that you didn't attend a historically black college because those officers don't do very well." Can you imagine being greeted that way as you start your military career? He credits his many years of training and preparation, as well as his deep-rooted faith, with getting him through the meeting without being upset. It was obvious that my husband had a trench to deal with, but by staying focused and committed to achieving his goals, he maintained his character and rose above the situation.

As usual, his hard work, attention to detail, and exceptional leadership qualities propelled him quickly to the top. At twenty-five years old, he was the youngest company commander at Ft. Sill. That's when the long hours began and the drift began to take place. As the days passed and my husband found himself working twelve to fifteen-hour days, we went through a time of distance. Although we spent as much time together as we could, a disconnect was taking place. As we spent more and more time apart, I found myself seeking solace in hanging out with other spouses who were having the same experience. Our communication, not to mention my dream to be a talk show host, was now on the back burner, and I found I had a lot of time on my hands.

This is when I found that I had to be the most attentive to my relationship because the theory is, "an idle mind will make idle hands get into mischief." *When you are not communicating and connecting with your spouse, it leaves the door open for something or someone else to try to wedge between you.* Because the tension existed, my husband said he found himself working later hours and not looking forward to coming home. This needed to be addressed quickly and nipped in the bud or it would have grown and caused an even greater distance between us. Misery loves company, as it has been shared down through the years, and of course, there are always those people looking for some gossip to share.

I remember one incident when my husband and I were working on spending more time together and decided to meet for lunch at a local drive-up eatery right outside the installation gate. We had both driven our cars and parked side by side. I joined him in his car while we enjoyed lunch and talked. When it was time to go, I leaned over and kissed him goodbye and got back into my car. Later that afternoon, one of my husband's colleagues came into his office to offer a word of advice. He told him that he should be more discreet if he was going to have an affair because he was seen at an eatery

> When you are not communicating and connecting with your spouse, it leaves the door open for something or someone else to try to wedge between you.

kissing a lady in his car. The lady, of course, was me. We learned early on that our lives were going to be viewed in a fishbowl and how easily people can be drawn into a mess at your expense if you're not aware.

No one sat me down and explained the culture of military life or the various protocols and the many sacrifices and unspoken rules. I was to just be a supportive spouse and attend functions, coffees, and game nights. I didn't have a mentor at that time to help me realize that my value was not attached to my husband's rank and that I had many skills and talents that would later open many doors for me. This would eventually have a huge impact on the lives of thousands of people over my thirty-five-year span as a military spouse. However, because of my faith walk, I had something to keep me grounded, and I recognized that I was an asset to my husband, as he was to me.

As I mentioned earlier, shortly after arriving at Ft. Sill, I had the wonderful opportunity to obtain a job as a reporter at the local TV station. I was finally moving forward toward my dream and began to feel the validation that I needed to use my gifts and talents. During that time, it was helpful that as my husband was serving as commander and was gone quite a bit, I was able to establish my purpose. Preserving my individual identity was so important to be a complete partner in my marriage.

Triumphant Thinking

1. Invest in yourself. Read books and information that will educate and equip you to adapt to the culture of a new lifestyle. This principle applies to anyone embarking upon a career that takes you into the political arena, or one that delves into the world of a Fortune 500 company. You must be aware and astute to stroll graciously and fit into your new lifestyle with confidence and knowledge.
2. Find a mentor. Be aware of those seasoned individuals you may be able to tap into. Don't be afraid to ask for help and guidance.

SECTION 2

Enduring The Struggle

When encountering difficulty or experiencing the unknown, I learned to give it the benefit of the doubt. The next four chapters express the highest level of character shaping: (1) "Battleground," (2) "Right Place - Wrong People," (3) "Advance or Retreat," and (4) "The Test."

CHAPTER 5

Battleground

Little did I know at this time that my husband was feeling the same disconnect. Later, in our marriage enrichment book, *It's Okay to Have an Affair (with Your Spouse)*, he revealed that he had gone to the door of the JAG (judge advocate general) office to inquire about the process for filing for a divorce. Yes, this was his thinking at the time, and I wasn't even aware of it. I eventually learned more about watching for what is not being said in your relationship to prevent some things from going too far.

He later shared that he had a spiritual encounter and a huge feeling of guilt as he stood on the doorstep of the Judge Advocate General (JAG) office, one that redirected him and gave him a new perspective on our relationship, which dramatically turned our marriage around. It takes both spouses to come to this conclusion for it to work. Never is it one-sided. The key is taking ownership of what you contribute to the relationship. I too had to step up to the plate.

As my husband was working diligently at bridging the emotional divide within our relationship, he decided he would surprise me by buying me a new car. What a wonderful gesture! But what he didn't realize was that his evenings coming home late and mystery conversations on the phone were not helping our situation.

Because the level of trust was still being built, I thought he was having an extramarital affair. I told one of my sisters-in-law, and she told my husband that he had better say something to me because his surprise was going to backfire. So he told me, and it did spoil the surprise, but it was the beginning of the unification in our relationship. Trust became the number-one factor, and it has been until this day.

I grew from that experience, realizing if I thought something was wrong, I needed to ask. Trust is very delicate, and I had to believe the best and not the worst.

It is difficult to admit that we are not perfect and that we could be the problem. No one ever wants to be called out and uncovered. We want the appearance that all is well. Both of us were very proud and held our character in the highest regard. We thought we lived lives that represented the best in a person. We loved, laughed, and showed the world that a good, solid marriage is possible. Of course, some didn't want our marriage to work and would have been happy to hear that we were finished. Our true love, faith, and determination sustained us. Much prayer and a lot of conversations, along with wise counsel from a few trusted couples who had been married longer than we had helped us to get through our struggles.

We attended a few marriage retreats and invested in literature and books to help us communicate better. Now, over thirty-six years later, we're standing strong and working daily to build a cohesive unit. It never stops. Our relationships with family and friends comprise a lifelong masterpiece, taking many different turns along the way.

Consistently, we decided to work at bringing our best selves to our relationship. Nevertheless, we still faced challenges and disappointments, but we remained committed to upholding our vows. Yes, those vows have been tested, but we're still here.

> It is difficult to admit that we are not perfect and that we could be the problem.

As our relationship was improving, unfortunately, tragedy struck. My mother passed away. I was twenty-seven years old and shocked. I walked around like I was in a fog, unable to see clearly. I moved through that period pretty much numb. My mother and I were best friends and had spent so much quality time together in a relationship where I seemed almost like an only child. I was the youngest of six and in the eighth grade when my last sibling left home and headed to California to live with my oldest sister just as the rest of my siblings had done. My mother and I spoke on the phone often, sometimes two or three times a day, and I would go home on weekends as much as I could.

Throughout my time living at home and while in college, I made it a point to be there for my mother. If she needed anything, she could call me and I was there. She taught me how to be a graceful woman and to be peaceful and compassionate and always be true to myself. Her great sense of humor kept us laughing and in tears most of the time we were together. When I was living out my rebellious ways, she always had my back. She was the go-between and negotiator with my dad.

> The battlefield of the mind is a fierce place, and without a way to regroup and refocus, you could absolutely lose your mind.

I remember one time in my senior year of high school. I had been given a curfew to attend a production cast party. But I decided I would stay out past the curfew. When I got home, my dad had barricaded the front door so that I could not get in. Of course, my loving mother was in bed still awake, waiting to get up to let me in.

We shared so many stories and late-night conversations about life and how proud she was of me, and how excited she was about my future. When she met my husband (then friend), she fell in love with him right away, and she always told me he was a good man. She knew he would take good care of me, she said. My mom's death was a wake-up call for me. I hadn't put trust in another person like that, and now I was truly vulnerable. The most precious memory that I hold dear occurred two weeks before she died when I came home for the weekend. We hugged and laughed and cried together at that time, not knowing it would be the last time I would see her.

The battlefield of the mind is a fierce place, and without a way to regroup and refocus, you could absolutely lose your mind. I have found that when facing a tragedy, unexpected or anticipated, my character would be tested, as well as my ability to rise out of the ashes. This major event helped me realize who I truly was.

Bounce-Back Mentality

This was a turning point in my life, bringing to bear everything that my mother had taught me. Going from calling my mother on the phone every day to realizing she was no longer there was a battle all in itself.

The trauma of this loss can't be put into words. I remember sobbing uncontrollably at the drop of a hat. Of course, I did this in the privacy of my home and when no one was around, because I was a strong woman, and I could handle anything, so I thought. But truly, it was the greatest loss I had ever experienced. You never know how important your mother is until she is no longer with you. She was my confidant, my "she-ro," my mentor and role model. She was such a graceful woman, with a quiet spirit, but a dynamite presence. A picture of her beautiful face, with her hazel-colored eyes, is etched in my memory, and the sound of her lovely soprano voice rings in my heart as I take my steps every day and breathe a new breath of life. Memories of cooking in the kitchen and reciting poetry to a little jig brought strength in my darkest hours.

To make matters worse and higher on the stress Richter scale, I was five months pregnant with our first child and beginning to deal with the reality that my mother would never meet my baby. Who would I ask questions about this pregnancy? What would I need to purchase to prepare before the baby came? What does the pain feel like, and how will I know what to do when the contractions start?

Over the years, I met many military spouses who had gone through this same experience in life without their mothers—and often without even their spouses—nearby. There were some whose mothers were not present in their lives and some who had strained relationships; thus making a support network even more critical. This is the time when other spouses become your family and step up to provide the support that you never knew could be possible, often from strangers. It is the unspoken rule that comes with being a fellow military spouse. We are all different, but the same. The camaraderie and esprit de corps stand strong in this unique unit of people. I discovered that I could trust and depend on them and they could depend on me as well, especially in times of trouble.

No matter what race, religion, culture, or background you come from, once that oath is taken to serve our country and to uphold the beliefs that serve all people, we are connected. Somehow, through the difficulty of it all, I decided I had to live on and provoke the tenacity from within that had been established in me since my early childhood. I could do anything with the strength of my faith and the love and support of my husband. I decided then that I had to focus my energies on carrying and birthing a healthy baby. I made a choice amid my grief, my trench.

Just as any family goes through its share of troubles and separations, we faced several different challenges at that time as well. My mother died the same day I resigned from my position at the TV station. When I resigned, I wasn't aware that she had passed. My plan was to spend some time with my mother, who was fighting bronchial asthma. It wasn't meant to be. If I had spent those last days observing her in pain, the experience might have had an irreversible impact on me emotionally.

What a turn of events. My life seemed to take on a whole new dimension as I realized that being a mother was the most important role that I could undertake. Now more than ever, I needed my relationship with my husband to work. It wasn't just about me now.

> No matter what race, religion, culture, or background you come from, once that oath is taken to serve our country and to uphold the beliefs that serve all people, we are connected.

Triumphant Thinking

1. Build upon every disappointment and turn it into a victory.
2. Allow your inner warrior to rise in times of despair and setbacks.
3. You are stronger than you think, and sometimes you have to prove it to yourself.

CHAPTER 6

Right Place – Wrong People

Soon after our first daughter was born, my husband received orders to attend the Officer Advanced Course at Aberdeen Proving Grounds in Maryland. This was a move that would take us to the East Coast, completely away from both of our families. During this time, I would depend on my strong upbringing and trust that I had everything I needed in me to face any challenge. Our first duty station felt like a military spouse boot camp and gave me additional tools for coping with life in the military. Now, I was about to face my first major challenge as a military spouse.

Behold, the Sandpaper People!

I was not ignorant of the evil forces that loom in the atmosphere and aware that not everyone will like you. Often, we are faced with individuals who are unhappy in their own lives, insecure, or just plain jealous of what your life presents. I was now faced with that one person I was just not going to win over. I soon realized, as Michelle Obama would say, that I had to go high when this person went low.

Behold, the Sandpaper People! I found out over the years that when I met someone whose spirit didn't agree with mine, they were intentionally placed in my life to sharpen me. I began to realize the importance of sandpaper and that there are different grades to be used for various purposes. Sandpaper is used mainly to change the texture of the surface of something. The roughness of its surface determines the grade of sandpaper needed to achieve the desired result. There is a proverb that says, "Iron sharpens iron," and just as a diamond must go through a process before its brilliance is shown, I too needed to go through a process to be the person I was created to be. This simple observation taught me that some people are like sandpaper. In other words, some people have been placed in my life to rub me in an irritating way, not to break me but to smooth out my rough edges, just like sandpaper does, bringing forth a refined and better product.

As a leader, I recognize opportunities to influence others and to guide them to a positive outcome in an endeavor. Being a leader brought additional responsibilities, challenges, and oppositions. I am a person who truly dislikes confrontation and will go above and beyond to avoid it. But I have also learned when sandpaper people show up in my life, they are intended to serve a purpose. Living triumphantly in the trenches is not just the title of the book; it is literally my life's story.

While my husband was going through the Advanced Course, he was the senior-ranking person in his class group, and therefore, he was also assigned to be the "mayor" of our living quarters area. While he was away for training, I had to deal with a sandpaper person in our neighborhood. The incident could have been dealt with differently, for sure, but it taught me a lesson nonetheless.

One afternoon, while my daughter, who was about eighteen months old at that time, was taking a nap, I suddenly heard really loud music coming from the garage of a neighbor's house. It startled me for a moment, and then I realized what it was. I figured it was the teenagers who often played there on the weekends. Of course, my daughter woke up startled, which annoyed me even further. I waited for about thirty minutes. Then, realizing it was not going to stop, I preceded to go down to ask if they could tone it down a bit.

First mistake: I should have addressed the issue with the parents, not the children. Dealing with other peoples' children can exacerbate a problem. I asked the young men if they could tone it down because my baby was napping and the response was, "No! We have every right to play here. It's daytime, and we can play for as long as we like."

Second mistake: I mentioned I would need to call the base police if they continued their behavior. Now they were really upset and becoming aggressive, so I went back to my house to make the call, and suddenly, there was a loud banging on my front door.

It was the parent of the teenager doing all of the back-talking. She spoke to me very disrespectfully, yelling and cursing that I was out of line and who did I think I was telling her son and friends to tone the music down. She had friends on the police force who would handle this, she said.

I tried to reason with her, explaining that I was not being malicious in my request, but she was not hearing any of it. This was the same woman with whom I'd had a conflict during our previous time there. The woman began to rant about how my husband and I thought we were all that and that just because we were the mayors of the area didn't mean a thing. Much more was said that I will not give credence to, but it was my first experience learning how to deal with a sandpaper person where I should have been experiencing a sense of camaraderie at its finest.

The music went on for a short time after, and my baby finally went back to sleep, but this was a very threatening situation. I had leveled up for sure, gaining new self-confidence and skill dealing with difficult people. This situation could happen to anyone anywhere, and that day, it could have had a very different outcome.

The threat of violence has increased significantly, and the lack of values within many families puts more people in an uncomfortable position to try to do the right thing. Each time we had to relocate, it became increasingly important to know the neighborhood and the challenges we might face. I often refer back to the "sandpaper people" analogy to keep me focused on the principle that I was being perfected for a greater purpose. Trust me when I say I encountered many sandpaper people over the years, and I'm sure I will encounter more in the future.

Depending on the branch of service, relocations may come frequently or space apart, but it is something you can count on. I had to be organized and detailed in my planning, from learning how to pack out a house to finding a new home in a new city to locating schools, grocery stores, a church home, a doctor, a dentist, as well as any community resources available to make the transition a little smoother for all. The key to being triumphant as I went through these various seasons was to have a "battle plan."

Once I experienced our first duty station and learned to navigate the use of the commissary and medical clinics, and the Family Readiness or Team Building resources, I was ready for anything that came my way. At least, that's what I thought. It is guaranteed that challenge, disappointment, and issues will come, but as I became resilient, I developed the ability to adapt quickly and get back on my feet whenever I got knocked down.

With each move, my husband requested a sponsor to help us acclimate to our new home and area. I requested a packet from the family support center that included all pertinent information within the community and a calendar of events held on the military installation. Even though I took steps to help in the relocation process, I could not alleviate the pressures and stresses that came along with it. I needed a plan of action to get through each move and to deal with the unknown. It took more than just having the information that gave me a better view of the new area. I also had real conversations with my spouse, addressing the reality of feeling overwhelmed and sometimes abandoned when having to make the move alone. Once again, I found myself in a place to create a home of love, safety, and security.

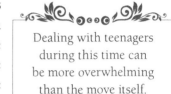

Dealing with teenagers during this time can be more overwhelming than the move itself.

Children are also affected by frequent moves and are forced to continuously adapt to new places, new friends, and new schools, as well as finding their place to belong. Sometimes, they act out at school, or they are verbally disrespectful to parents as a means of expressing their stress or fear.

Dealing with teenagers during this time can be more overwhelming than the move itself. This is when I really began to listen to my children, hearing what was being said as well as what was not being said. As an adult, we typically adjust and move on. We internalize our fears and concerns, whereas most children haven't developed that skill yet. I had many friends who had horrific experiences with their families during the period of transition. It was critical to ensure everyone had a safe place to express what was going on in their minds. I felt this was truly critical, as suicide was becoming one of the top leading causes of death in teens between the ages of twelve and nineteen.

Triumphant Thinking

1. Allow challenge to strengthen your resolve. The outcome is a testament to who you are and the caliber of your character.
2. The sandpaper people are placed in your life intentionally. Allow the process to refine you.
3. Keep communication open with your children as you experience change together.
4. Listen for what is not being said.

CHAPTER 7

Advance or Retreat— It's Your Choice

New doors opened following advanced officer training as my husband was selected to attend Babson College to obtain a master's degree in business administration. This was the next big step for our family. We had to adjust to a different climate and possible job choices, as well as adjust to no longer living on a military installation, where a young family still trying to navigate their relationship could find the resources they needed and achieve their individual and collective goals.

Making the best of every move and situation, no matter how it looked, was my specialty. For the first few months, I had to accept the stay-at-home mom role and to support my husband as he was consumed with a very demanding course load. Not long into the spring semester, another incident challenged us. While playing basketball, my husband ruptured his Achilles tendon. The pressures were now even stronger as I had to keep a positive outlook, encourage my husband, take care of our daughter, and still try to find my place of validation as an individual. Had I not been wired to be triumphant in the trenches, I would have thought my life to be merely one incident happening after another, like some kind of curse. The truth is, life just happens. No one gets a free pass. It had become clear to me that normally a setback was just a set-up for an upcoming victory in my life.

What we do with the situations we are dealt with determines how we move on in our future.

What we do with the situations we are dealt with determines how we move on in our future.

My need to be *triumphant in the trenches* developed at every turn. Facing and winning battles in my life was part of the perfecting process. Resiliency was paramount to building the wall within the trench to make sure it was solid and wouldn't collapse during a challenge along my life's journey.

The nearest installation was Hansom Air Force Base. It was not realistic to seek employment that required a long-distance drive each way. Connecting within the community YMCA, I found a preschool for my daughter and started to build a network of friends to help me settle in. A great door opened when we found out that there was housing available at a small military base called Natick Labs Training Center. Soon after moving into quarters there, I was offered a position as an assistant manager of the small post exchange store, which meant I could walk to work from my home. This was when I started to feel validated and able to contribute financially to the wellbeing of our family. Understand that up to now, my contribution as a dedicated wife and mother had been substantial in the unity and success of our family, but I still needed more to feel I was living with purpose. Remember, I'm a people person, and I drew strength from assisting others. Where we draw our strength varies from person to person.

This opportunity led to another door opening for me to show the power of love and how we are all in need of care and appreciation. A soldier from a local unit who specialized in testing special warfare gear was being sent to the Gulf War. He had newly married and his spouse, who was Korean, did not speak English well. I promised to help her and offered her a job in the store, stocking shelves. This was one of the greatest character-shaping opportunities in my life. I taught her English, taught her how to drive, and promoted her to a cashier while her husband was deployed for seven months. This period was not without significant challenges, but I loved my job and had a good overall rapport with most of the customers. However, a few people expressed their disdain for me and my employee. Yes, the sandpaper-person syndrome. This was evident as they would not speak to or acknowledge us when we spoke to them and some would even throw their money on the counter. I was determined not to allow this to discourage me or change my character. No matter how bad the situation became, I made up in my mind that I would stand my moral ground and not give in to my emotions.

During these experiences, I was stretched once again, this time to endure a sort of prejudice I had never experienced. In life, I dealt with various situations calmly and moved on without saying anything or addressing them. However, as I have written and revisited each aspect of my journey, I remember how painful those instances were. I believe

I had the power to change my environment and affect the lives of those I touched each day if I stayed true to who I was

I had buried the hurt and disappointment fearing it would overtake me and change me. It did change me, but it changed me for the better. I came to recognize the fact that those who didn't know me feared me and were empty in their skins dealing with their insecurities. I chose to show the difference and the power of love and acceptance, no matter what the situation looked like.

When it was time for us to relocate to the next station, something very special happened. During my farewell luncheon and celebration, the Base Commander honored and recognized my contributions that had improved the exchange and taken it to the next level while under my management. Some of the people celebrating and giving me praise wouldn't even speak to me the year prior. It was clearly evident to me, more than ever before, that *I had the power to change my environment and affect the lives of those I touched each day if I stayed true to who I was* and lived triumphantly in the trenches.

My life had new meaning. That's what happens when you take your eyes off your circumstance and find the courage to help someone who needs you. Maybe I was not able to follow my first dream to become a broadcast journalist, but now, new dreams were taking shape and with just as much meaning and accomplishment. I embraced my circumstances instead of allowing them to destroy me.

My next growth experience occurred at my husband's graduation and deciding to let our daughter, now three years old, go back to Oklahoma with my husband's parents. I had never allowed her to stay with anyone more than a night and this would be for two weeks. It wasn't that I didn't trust my in-laws, but as a mother with her only child, I was super cautious and it wouldn't have mattered who it was that I had to trust for that amount of time.

I have always encouraged parents to use wisdom and discernment when it comes to their children and who they allow to become a part of their inner circle. I realized that I couldn't trust everyone and not everyone possessed the same moral compass as my husband and me. We were accountable for our decisions, and I had to be okay with our choices.

I could only perceive how others lived and their perceived standards might not have met my expectations. In many cases, those feelings may have been unfounded, but stories I had heard of violence and mistreatment of children when their parents were not around and it gave me pause and concern. We survived, and it was a great opportunity for our daughter to connect with her grandparents and create memories.

Triumphant Thinking

1. A setback is really just a setup for an upcoming victory in your life.
2. Don't get too hung up on yourself. Focus on helping others.
3. Trenches and opportunity show you who you really are. They build character.
4. No matter how difficult your life is, someone else is worse off.

CHAPTER 8

The Test

After completing the master's program at Babson, the question was "Where to next?" What would be the best career move? Surprisingly, we were headed to the Republic of Panama.

The distance from family was becoming greater as we maneuvered through this active duty journey. Moving away from family and friends is one of the key components of growing closer together and learning to depend on your core beliefs and the unique military community. The question of whether I could find employment was now starting to become paramount. I was excited about the opportunity to live overseas and to experience a new culture. I studied Spanish in high school and had not done much with it since then. Here was the perfect time to refresh and stretch. Not only was I searching for my purpose, but I also started thinking about the possibility of going back to school. Maybe this would be a good time to continue my education while looking for a job.

Thankfully, I was offered a position with the AAFES (Army Air Force Exchange Services) Facilities Operations for Vendors. This helped my mental state. It was a chance to improve my Spanish speaking ability and to build my resume as a military spouse. The research for online schools and for a field of study I wanted to pursue was in motion.

In the first few months, I stayed busy maintaining my home and helping our daughter adjust to a new country and culture. My next sandpaper challenge was dealing with a military spouse who ended up working with and for me in the video rental store. Because we were neighbors, she felt she had some inside relation that would give her priority and favor on the job. This put a strain on the otherwise great relationship we had enjoyed. I found that the choice to keep my personal life separate from my professional one was taxing and emotional. It's unfortunate that in relationships, there must always be boundaries and clear expectations or someone will be hurt, disappointed, or misunderstood.

Most people are looking for the WIIFM ("What's in it for me?") and not considering the other person and what they may want as well. This mindset is very selfish, and in marriage, it is a deal-breaker. Becoming who we were created to be takes a lot of time, experience, flexibility, and inner soul-searching to make sure we are developing the character traits and strong moral compass we need to be a decent human being.

Interestingly, my husband's job required each of the officers to spend a six-month deployment rotation at Joint Task Force-Bravo in Honduras. My husband was due to start his deployment rotation when I was eight and a half months pregnant with our second child. His senior rater was not going to show favoritism and told my husband he had to go and could come back on leave after the baby was born. Needless to say, my husband was not happy, and unsuccessfully tried to come up with alternatives on his own. But thanks be to God, one of his colleagues showed compassion and volunteered to go until two weeks after our son was born.

The six-month deployment rotation turned into nine months due to unforeseen circumstances with the position as the officer that was scheduled to deploy next accepted the Army's "Early-out" bonus. When my husband finally returned, our son had just started walking. Our baby boy looked at my husband as a stranger for a while, but after months of loving on him and lots of playtimes, they bonded. This scenario was too familiar with the spouses in my friend group. We intentionally formed a support system for each other.

During my husband's nine-month absence, I was forced to grow in areas that I had previously depended on my husband for support only to realize I could handle more responsibility than I had in the past. I had also acquired another new responsibility with the chapel service I attended. These wonderful and loving parishioners unquestionably helped me become more stable as a young mother and military spouse. I remain grateful to them to this day. It was essential and very beneficial for me to find a group I could connect with.

At various times in life, you may experience a season of feeling disjointed and maybe even lost. Often I asked myself what my purpose was and what I should be accomplishing at that time. Being a mother gave me a sense of purpose and accomplishment, but I also needed to feel complete in my desire to achieve my personal goals. Understanding the dynamics and timing of pursuing a career, along with taking care of my family, was paramount to accomplishing both.

Sometimes, the challenges we face are placed there intentionally to grow us in an area that needs improvement.

Interacting with all types of people has been a key strength I have possessed all of my life. I didn't appreciate how important this skill was until later. Every challenge and sandpaper experience I had was making me stronger, more resilient, and more humble.

Sometimes, the challenges we face are placed there intentionally to grow us in an area that needs improvement. By embracing the obstacles and learning to find solutions, I developed skills necessary to live a full, victorious life—in other words, to be triumphant in the trenches.

I learned to run toward the opposition with full courage and strength, knowing I was already equipped to win. Trust me, this "mind-itude" (a word I created, meaning the transformation of one's mind and attitude) didn't occur overnight. This process was and is still ongoing. The dictionary defines attitude as "a position assumed for a specific purpose; a mental position with regard to a fact or a state." My position was to take control of my situation, and although there were many sleepless nights, tear-stained pillows, and long dialogues with mentors, I was determined to develop this state of mind.

Life was moving along very well now, as I was getting adjusted to being a mother of two, working, and keeping the home front balanced with help from a part-time nanny. Then, another tragedy hit! My oldest brother was accidentally shot and killed in a gang-related drive-by shooting in Northern California. He was coaching at a little league baseball practice, and when he had returned to his car to get baseball bats and gear from the trunk of his car, he was struck by a stray bullet. During a full-on chase of some individuals who had jumped the fence of the baseball field and fled through the parking lot, they were firing at one another when my brother was struck and killed.

How devastating this incident was. The loss of a loved one is difficult no matter how it happens, but this knocked me off my feet. My big brother was jovial, loving, smart, and clever. His smile and deep, raspy voice are as strong in my memory now as they were the last time I saw him alive. The trench in this situation affected not only me but my entire family on a whole new level. He left behind a wife and three daughters, and this happened on the birthday of his oldest daughter. I've often thought about how this affected them and how they could move on with their lives. There were no clear answers, but because this, unfortunately, was not a new experience for me, I knew that grief was a process and that each of us would deal with it in our own way and according to our own timing. This was just another season of trenches to somehow get through triumphantly.

So now what? I'm thousands of miles from California, and my husband has just returned from Honduras with pneumonia and too sick to travel. Do I stay or do I go? Life had just thrown me another curveball, and once again, I had to pull from my internal fortitude to push ahead despite the situation. My husband convinced me to go to California for the funeral service for my brother, as he had enough friends who would make sure he was taken care of while I was away.

So the journey began across the seas and country, with two small children, to face another serious emotional battle alone. This is what military spouses do: face trenches head-on. I was not sure how I would make it through this one. How would I experience victory while being encompassed in the emotional ditch that had been dug around my mind to help me survive another battle? Someone said, "What does not kill us makes us stronger." That statement rang true long before it was recorded in a song.

Timing Is Everything!

"What does not kill you makes you stronger!"

Although these lyrics have become familiar from a secular song but it was initially noted by a German author named, Friedrich Nietzsche, and the truth of the statement is powerful! How do you soar above the obstacles and challenges that attempt to halt your progress as you pursue your dreams? For me, it meant being tenaciously persistent with dignity.

I believe we were created with a deep desire to achieve, to express uniqueness, and to make contributions to our communities. As we travel through life to the places where we fulfill our destiny, the journey and transformation become part of our growth process. Where is your journey taking you? What trench or roadblocks are you facing? What's your plan of attack, and how will you implement it? We don't tend to think about this regularly because we are so busy living life. But I found that it is essential to achieving a vibrant and fulfilling life.

"What does not kill you makes you stronger!"

I believe before we even existed, our paths were already established. There are no challenges we are not already equipped to handle. Yes, I can acquire more skills and abilities to help me deal with the vicissitudes of life, but I know that I have what it takes to be triumphant regardless of my circumstances.

There appears to have been a perfect time set, as I have taken that step into my destiny. I have faced disappointments and delays, but the intentional plan for my life will not be thwarted. It only happens if I allow it to. *Don't give anyone or anything the power to hinder you in completing your mission.*

The four natural seasons come and go, and with each one, there are distinct characteristics that make them recognizable. Sometimes variants occur that are confusing and cause me to think, "This isn't normal for this season." In the pursuit of my dreams, I have found myself saying this same thing concerning each season. The struggle is part of the process, and there is an appointed season for greatness to come to fruition. I truly believe that whenever we experience a great

> Don't give anyone or anything the power to hinder you in completing your mission.

setback, we are on the verge of obtaining our greatest victory. I had to encourage myself many times to be steadfast in my journey and stay the course. However, sometimes, it felt as though the walls of the trench were about to cave in.

Triumphant Thinking

1. Connecting with a support group is essential.
2. Challenge promotes growth if you can handle it.
3. Stay the course. It's what you attain at the end that brings the most joy.
4. Get a new "mind-itude." Change how you think about your circumstances. What you visualize is what you bring into existence.

SECTION 3
Growth Tactics

Growing pains never feel good, but what tests you the most in your investment brings out the greatest return. Although (1) "The Impact of Loss" may be substantial, many times there is (2) "The Unexpected Gift" that brings faith into perspective while (3) "Life-Changing Experiences" prepare you for (4) "The Test for the Next Level."

CHAPTER 9

The Impact of Loss

We completed the tour in the Republic of Panama and were now on our way to a one-year assignment in Atlanta, Georgia. My husband's MBA was now coming into use as he was going to experience working with a prominent defense contractor called Rockwell International, under the sponsorship of the army's Training with Industry program. I had never been to Atlanta before and was somewhat apprehensive about moving to the South in light of many incidents that had occurred related to race and cultural differences. I had never experienced any major issues of this nature, and I was not looking for any now.

This was an eye-opening experience for a small-town girl who had been protected from much of the ugliness in the world because I was sheltered by my parents and family. Being a people person, I never met a stranger and always embraced people for just being people, regardless of their race, religion, nationality, etc.

We searched for a few weeks to find a home suitable and within a reasonable distance to work, school, and amenities for our now-growing family. To my surprise, I soon found out that a close childhood friend I grew up with did not live far from me. We connected, and what a joy that was. She also had two adorable young daughters. After only a few short months, we realized how much we had in common and ignited a lifelong relationship. We would have dinners together, go shopping with our children, and just be there to provide a great support system for one another.

I realized nothing happened by chance and that I was being guided and my footsteps were being ordered. Within six months of reconnecting this wonderful friendship, another tragedy struck. My dear friend's husband was diagnosed with cancer, and soon after, he passed away. Although I had recently experienced the death of a loved one and could remember how devastated I was, this was not like any emotion I had ever experienced.

This was my first true introduction to dealing with a close friend's grief. Why did this affect me this way at this time? Maybe because it was a close friend and it had happened so unexpectedly. Over the years, several of my friends, both civilian and military, lost loved ones, and I had firsthand experience with the challenges they faced to move on with their lives. Grief is an area that is a big challenge for most people. What I learned is that there are varying degrees of grief, and everyone processes it differently. Some people can simply adjust and move on quickly, and others may never overcome it.

> three T's: time, talking, and tears. Allow these to take their course as you heal.

Please understand that grief can be experienced for other reasons besides the loss of a loved one. The loss of a job, income, status, relationship, health, community/church, or home can lead to grief. Our identity is connected and wrapped up in so many things that we endure each day, and it can be hugely impactful when there is a change, whether gradual or sudden, and unexpected. The impact this has on an individual can be very grave, and have a ripple effect among our family and those around us. I discovered how important it is to deal with loss, disappointment, or any change in circumstance as quickly as possible so that it does not have a lingering negative impact.

Expressing my true feelings has helped me navigate through the process. Grief affects everyone differently, and not everyone can share how it affects him or her. A friend gave me a great piece of advice concerning grief as I was suffering through it. She told me about *the three T's: time, talking, and tears. Allow these to take their course as you heal.*

I hope that sharing this wonderful information that assisted me in dealing with grief will also provide some comfort for those who may need it. This was gleaned from a study by Kubler-Ross, on the various stages of grief, which are denial, anger, bargaining, depression, and acceptance. I will share the pertinent points, but please do your own detailed research if you find yourself dealing with grief. I have shared this information with many and continue to learn and build on it as needed. Although I'll present these in the order listed above, sometimes you may experience them in a different order.

The Five Stages of Grief by Kubler-Ross

Denial

Denial is the first of the five stages of grief. It helps us to survive the loss. In this stage, the world becomes meaningless and overwhelming. Life makes no sense. We are in a state of shock and denial. Denial and shock help us to cope and make survival possible. As you accept the reality of the loss, you are unknowingly beginning the healing process. You are becoming stronger, and the denial is beginning to fade. But as you proceed, all the feelings you were denying begin to surface.

Anger

Anger is a necessary stage of the healing process. Be willing to feel your anger, even though it may seem endless. The truth is that anger has no limits. It can extend not only to your friends, the doctors, your family, yourself, and your loved one who died but also to God. You may ask, "Where is God in this?" Underneath anger is pain, your pain. We usually know more about suppressing anger than feeling it. The anger is just another indication of the intensity of your love.

Bargaining

Before a loss, it seems as if you would do anything to spare your loved one. We become lost in a maze of "If only ..." or "What if ?" statements. We want life returned to what it was; we want our loved one restored. We may even bargain with the pain. We will do anything not to feel the pain of this loss. We remain in the past, trying to negotiate our way out of the hurt. We do not enter and leave each stage in a linear fashion. We may experience one stage of grief, move on to another for a time, and then revisit the previous one.

Depression

After bargaining, our attention moves squarely into the present. Empty feelings present themselves, and grief enters our lives on a deeper level, deeper than we had ever imagined. It's important to understand that this depression is not a sign of mental illness. It is the response to a great loss. We withdraw from life, left in a fog of intense sadness, wondering, perhaps, if there is any point in going on alone? Depression after a loss is too often seen as unnatural. The loss of a loved one is a very depressing situation, and depression is a common response. To not experience depression after a loved one dies would be unusual. If grief is a process of healing, then depression is one of the many steps along the way.

Acceptance

Acceptance is often confused with the notion of being "all right" or "okay" with what has happened. This stage is about accepting the reality that our loved one is physically gone and recognizing that this new reality is permanent. As we begin to live again and enjoy our life, we often feel that in doing so, we are betraying our loved one. We can never replace what has been lost, but we can make new connections, new meaningful relationships, new interdependencies. We begin to live again, but we cannot do so until we have given grief its time.

There are more stages of grief that can surface, and sometimes a person will experience all or maybe only a few of these. They may not happen in this order, and this has been examined and redefined over the last few years. I just wanted to share something to give someone hope and to validate what many military families go through in their time of service to our country. Time has a way of healing hurts and disappointments. It is only when we allow it to work in our lives that we can benefit from it. Just know that many other resources can assist. If you need help, get it.

Triumphant Thinking

1. Appreciate the people who are strategically placed in your life. You may not know why initially, but it is on purpose.
2. Faith is an agent in assisting us to get through some of the toughest times we must face. Grow strong in yours daily. You'll never know when you will need it most.
3. When encountering grief, whether it is the loss of a loved one or a shift in your life's status, allow it to take its natural course over time. Seek help, if needed.

CHAPTER 10

The Unexpected Gift

Our next assignment would take us to Fort Bragg, North Carolina, which brought many mixed emotions. I had to leave a dear friend in the process of dealing with the loss of her husband and picking up the pieces of her life to move on, which she did in time, in stellar form.

Being assigned to Fort Bragg, and more specifically the 82d Airborne Division brought new adventures and challenges. As the first certified contingency contracting officer in the division, my husband spent the majority of his time developing procedures for rapid deployment. To add to the stress level, he found himself running back and forth between Division G4 and the Division Support Command (DISCOM). Adding to his already busy and demanding day, he still had to stay at the top of his physical game, doing morning runs and strapping on a parachute to jump out of a perfectly good airplane. Okay, maybe nearly perfect.

The struggle to balance home and work is always present.

The struggle to balance home and work is always present.

Here we are, in the throes of purchasing our first home, which we were having built from the ground up. This was a perfect reflection of the foundation for our marriage—trust, flexibility, teamwork, and compromise. If you have never gone through this process, it can make or break your marriage. Our blueprint was growing stronger and clearer as we moved into the next season of our journey together. Although I was busy with two children and trying to keep up with their school and extracurricular activities, I still needed something for myself. I found comfort in volunteering with Army Family Team Building, and I realized I had a knack for teaching and facilitating. This helped me balance my time with the kids and gave me something valuable to contribute to.

Three months into this assignment, Army Forces Command (FORSCOM) handpicked my husband to deploy to Doha, Qatar in the Middle East for six months. The timing was crazy because we were still in the middle of unpacking and beautifying our new home.

When my husband returned from the Middle East, he took a break from jumping out of airplanes and went to Virginia to attend a professional development government contracting course. Then, yet another test occurred. My husband ruptured his other Achilles tendon while playing basketball. I thought I guess he didn't learn his lesson the first time. How could this be? The answer is, life just happens.

With every step forward, there seemed to be one that would take us backward. This could have been an opportunity to get on the pity-party bandwagon pretty quickly, seeing that we were just getting into a good routine and starting to rebuild my resume and skillsets. I had to take time out and focus my attention on the health of my home and family. I could have felt a bit resentful that, once again, my goals were being put on the backburner, but I was too busy to give it any credence.

During the tour at Fort Bragg, in particular, I realized how important it was to share my wisdom and skills at navigating this military lifestyle as a spouse. There were so many young spouses dealing with the unique atmosphere that comes with being in a military setting. This was a great time to help build solid homes with spouses and providing a solid emotional state that each of them needed.

Many wives were experiencing depression, addiction, alcoholism, adultery, and abandonment. How could I help these hurting, desperate women? By reaching out and inviting them to attend the support groups established to provide hope in hopeless situations. The counseling centers, the chaplain, and programs like Strong Bonds and PREP (Prevention and Relationship Enhancement Program) were available to assist couples and families. I was very engaged in these programs as a volunteer and gained a tremendous amount of skills and knowledge.

Dealing with deployments that ranged anywhere from six to

eighteen months brought great strain. Each waking day, you wondered if your spouse would return if your children still had a father or mother. None of these issues were mentioned in the headlines or addressed to help those left on the home front. As a spouse, I had access to great programs, such as Military One Source, the Chaplaincy, and Veterans Affairs, which were paramount in helping many of us get through this season of our lives.

Sometimes, amid these circumstances, it would have been easy to lose focus on what was important and lose hope. It was overwhelming at times making sure the bills were paid and the children were safe, both emotionally and physically. I learned that I was much stronger than I knew. The next season of my life definitely proved that.

Rearing a son was quite different from rearing our first daughter, who was driven, self-sustaining, and running on autopilot. My son was my greatest test and greatest growth factor. His high energy and never-ending ability to get into something kept me on my knees. Literally, I was scrubbing something all the time.

One memory that I hold dear was a lesson in not putting too high a price on things. We had just moved into our new home, and I had selected some very elegant off-white wallpaper for the entryway. It had a swirled pattern in it that, when the light hit just right from the chandelier, made it seem as if angels of light were dancing on the walls. Well, my son thought he would try to capture their silhouettes by tracing them with red, yellow, and blue crayons. Yeah, that didn't turn out so well. I was livid! This gift of a human life kept me constantly asking what I needed to do to help him settle down and act "normal." The truth is, I was growing up and learning that we are different and have various gifts and talents; we must be allowed to develop in our own ways.

There were days I thought I was going to pull out all my hair dealing with this boy. I would ask other mothers if they were experiencing the same struggles, and many of them said no. This left me to fend, read, and research to find answers that I could later share with other mothers who were going through some of the same challenges.

A great team of women who also poured into my life gave me the boost to move forward and step into a new phase of my destiny. I was asked to join the leadership team as part of the Army Family Team Building, and I was sent to Atlanta, Georgia, for the Master Trainer course. I may have been dislocated from my academic vocation as a reporter and journalist, but I was now being directed into the next steps toward my future. I was starting to gain momentum again, doing something that I loved and was pretty good at.

I had barely gotten the words out of my mouth when tragedy struck again. My oldest sister (eighteen years older than me) passed away in her sleep. She was fifty-four years old and had six daughters, and her youngest was thirteen at the time. What was going on here? The trenches seemed to be coming closer together and getting deeper. I was the youngest in my family, and my sister was like a second mother to me. She had left her children at home in California to come to Oklahoma when my first child was born. Who would stand in the gap for her daughters and be the mother figure they would need? This was mindboggling, and because I was not in a position to go to Oklahoma to live, my assistance would be only from a distance and infrequent at best. The loss of my sister took a toll on me. The only relief I could get in this situation was the next enormous blessing, which came unexpectedly.

Try planning your life and then enjoy a good laugh, because it is rarely what you expect.

Try planning your life and then enjoy a good laugh, because it is rarely what you expect. The next enormous blessing came when I gave birth to my youngest daughter. Now, I might have felt a little despondent at this time, seeing how I was thirty-six years old and not planning to have another child, but this was an ordained plan for my life especially since I had just lost my oldest sister.

I made an astonishing observation as I realized that with each loss of my family member, I had been given a child of the same sex as the one I had lost. This gave me such great peace and a sense of purpose for their lives. I didn't understand how the laws of life were working or how they were lining up to bring me into my destiny, but I did believe something greater than myself was guiding me through life. It gave me hope and a keen perspective.

My children are all about five years apart, and just when I had the one ready for full-day kindergarten, thinking I would have time to myself to focus by either furthering my education or getting a full-time job, things would change. I know how frustrating it can be if you are ready to move in a certain direction concerning your career and it comes to an abrupt halt. As a military spouse, this can become the norm, and some can't handle it or choose not to. When I stepped back to view the situation, I found that something greater and bigger than my aspirations was about to take place. The lessons I have learned so far were designed to force me to pause, reflect, and grow.

As I paused for a moment, I recognized that everything that had been shared with me over the many years, were key nuggets I should share with others because my life has been impacted for the better.

Triumphant Thinking

1. We all experience loss at some time. Knowing where to go for help will assist you in getting you through it (e.g., the stages of grief and counseling).
2. When your plans seem to fail, you redirect, because that was not the direction you were meant to go in anyway.

CHAPTER 11

A Life-Changing Experience

Believe it or not, we were now about to make our tenth move in thirteen years. Our lives were greatly affected when we received orders to move to Louisville, Kentucky. We weren't going to Fort Knox or Fort Campbell, to our surprise. My husband was assigned as the commander for a defense contract management office in Louisville, at a small privatized naval base.

The home search began once again as we toured the city and multiple communities to find the right fit. Our initial plan, stay in a hotel for a couple of weeks, became an extended stay as our five-month-old baby girl broke out in chickenpox. We later learned that she had been exposed to the disease five weeks earlier, while we were still in Fort Bragg, North Carolina.

We found an older home nestled in the corner of a cul-de-sac of an established neighborhood. The day we were moving in, a gentleman who lived at the end of the street walked down, kindly welcomed us, and offered to help navigate the movers, since I was busy keeping up with my son and youngest daughter—a handful itself. The man offered to have his wife fix dinner for us that evening without even asking her, which began a unique lifelong relationship. These two people were undoubtedly divinely placed in our lives.

Before we closed on our home, we noticed some not-so-nice graffiti that had been sprayed on the "stop" sign at the corner of our street. I was uncomfortable and concerned about whether this was the best place to live. My husband was emphatic that it was and that the graffiti was just a sign that *we were definitely in the right place, at the right time.*

It doesn't matter how good or kind you think you are. There are those in the world who, for whatever reason, are not happy with their lives and ultimately don't want you to be happy either. The camaraderie we experience in the confines of the military lifestyle pushed us past nationality, race, and religious preferences and built a sense of acceptability for those who put their lives on the line for all people.

The couple that came that day changed our lives and renewed our belief in mankind. Once again, we knew that if we look for the best in people, we can find it. It also confirmed our belief that if you treat others right, you will be treated right. It may not happen immediately, but we looked for and anticipated the return on our investment. That return came from the woman who fixed dinner for us on our first day in the neighborhood. She became a dear friend and confidant, a mentor who invited me to the women's study group that established a new path in my life. It strengthened me in my daily living and encouraged me, as a mother and a woman, in my life for eternity. This study group was established worldwide, and I was able to find it wherever I lived, even overseas. It was a turning point for me in my personal development and allowed me to rekindle my passion for facilitation.

> we were definitely in the right place, at the right time.

Making connections like this was paramount to sustaining my sanity and self-esteem. No matter where we come from, we all deal with life's disappointments and need someone to lean on in times of difficulty. This group helped me to build a network of other spouses who were experiencing similar challenges and struggles, providing an outlet and resources to aid in every area of my life.

Our two years in Kentucky provided opportunities to build relationships with mentors who have, to this day, profited us immensely. The spiritual, emotional, and professional guidance we have received over the years cannot be comprehended or adequately described. I owe a great deal of who I am today to those precious women and men who poured into our lives. As a military spouse and one whose mother passed away when I was pregnant with my first child, I had a void in my life that only a mother could fill and that only another woman could understand. I found that person, and she became my godmother over twenty years ago.

The most valuable lessons I learned were sometimes the ones that brought tears and hard work. Gaining a mentor was the most beneficial thing that could have happened in my life, and I had to be willing to accept the truth about myself and to listen to the sound advice that was provided to continue to grow into the person I am today.

Triumphant Thinking

1. Never allow the fears or ignorance displayed by someone else to detour you from your destiny.
2. Believe that wherever you go, someone will be there to affect your life positively.
3. Adversity will bring out the best or the worst in you.

CHAPTER 12

Test for the Next Level (Northern Virginia)

Should I go back to school or stay at home and make sure our children were stable and had a solid foundation? This question was posed with each new assignment but always seemed to have the same answer: family first.

My youngest was now almost two years old and as smart as a whip, carrying on full-fledged conversations and learning the basics to begin reading. I was starting to fidget a bit because I still yearned to be in the workforce, using my degree or at least sharpening the skills I had recently gained as a master trainer with Army Family Team Building. I did some soul-searching and chose to keep those dreams and desires at bay for a little while longer, so I needed to come up with an alternative plan.

So, as many other spouses did, I created income from home. I started a before-and-after school program that would assist other working mothers and provide a safe environment for their children so they could pursue their dreams of working outside the home. This could have been by design or necessity, but I saw a need and took advantage of the opportunity. I would see their children off to school, either walking them to the bus stop or dropping them off myself. This helped fill the gap, using my skills and love for nurturing and mentoring children, and it provided a little extra spending money and a sense of fulfillment.

One's self-esteem plays a huge part in how one succeeds in the role of a wife, a mother, or simply an individual. Let's not confuse confidence with self-esteem, because I was very confident in who I was and in my skills and abilities, but I was also honest with myself that I needed some validation as well. Most people never really address this challenge for fear of being found out, but I realized that being truthful with myself was the only way I would be successful in my relationships, seeing that I had to establish new ones every twenty to twenty-four months.

Watching my spouse go off to conquer the world each day, enjoying meaningful adult conversation and accomplishing the tasks at hand for the day, sometimes didn't compare to doing laundry, cleaning the house, and wiping dirty faces. However, I found that the more I focused on the end result—happy, healthy, and whole children—the more I found my days to be bearable and rewarding. I found that the choice to give my time and energy to my children, and others' children at that time, was teaching me more than I would ever know. The payoff would be far greater than my temporary feeling of lack of validation.

There are no true reasons why you haven't obtained your goals, only excuses.

What tips can I provide if you are in this situation?

First, you must be honest with yourself and then figure out what you need to help you get through this season of your life. When I took my children to the library and on field trips to enhance their early knowledge of the world and its possibilities, I would search for books and articles that challenged my thinking and inspirational ones to refresh my hope.

I observed something as I saw other spouses achieving their goals and dreams that had similar lifestyles. My path was what I made of it. *There are no true reasons why you haven't obtained your goals, only excuses.* Yes, if I could go back and do some things over, I would only adjust them, not totally change them, because those specific choices I made then are ones that helped shape who I am today.

Watching your children develop through the various stages of life from toddler to preteen to teenager and young adult, is so rewarding and, yes, sometimes very frustrating. These were years of learning and developing strategies to help my children navigate their life's journey. Of the three, my son was the measuring stick for my growth as a mother.

My daughters have also taught me great lessons but in different ways. My son was the iron that sharpens iron. He kept me humble and on my toes all the time. Spoiler alert: he is now a professional actor. So the work does pay off.

Rearing children who are gifted, bright, and intelligent can be daunting, and sometimes you feel you are not equipped to guide them to fulfill their destiny. This is where I found out what I was made of, and so I began the search for educational aids, books, and resources to ensure I was helping my children succeed and stay at the top of their academic levels. I didn't know it at the time, but this would be my saving grace. I began to add homeschooling to complement their school's curriculum and discovered I was good at teaching and explaining concepts at their level.

Many of my friends had degrees (including Masters and PhDs) in various disciplines and were also choosing to stay home to invest in their children. This was encouraging and provided adult conversation that sometimes was so desperately needed.

My husband and I built strong relationships with our church family and neighbors who encouraged us to grow as a couple and as individuals. Being able to share similar life's challenges proved profitable, as we received guidance concerning our children, who were now experiencing their own individual challenges and adjusting to moving once again. Our oldest daughter was now in middle school, our son was in elementary, and our youngest was a preschooler.

My energy shifted to providing the best experiences and opportunities possible for my children, and so began our busy life schedule. Piano lessons, Boy Scouts, travel basketball, and maintaining our home. How did we do it all? Being consistent, staying on task and focused on the priorities at the time, and not losing sight of our individual dreams and goals in the midst of it all.

This was the most critical time for shaping our oldest daughter, as she was approaching high school and starting to think about her interests and talents. She was brilliant, finishing as the valedictorian of her fifth-grade class, and she has her name on the wall of that school in Kentucky. She was an MVP (most valuable player) basketball star and a classical pianist, and at age twelve, she had the most beautiful voice, bigger than just singing the national anthem a few times at school. We were now focused on what would set our daughter up for success and ensure her dreams were obtainable. Ideally, we hoped she would be able to attend the college of her choice.

Our son, now a second-grader and already a phenomenal drummer, was still adjusting to school and learning how to sit down and be still for longer than five minutes. This is where my greatest lessons in rearing a boy developed. As a parent, I didn't have a "101" lesson plan telling me how to deal with each child. They are individuals with different needs and different gifts and talents, and each of them needs your undivided attention to arrive at the best place in life for the child and for you. Sometimes, that is a lot easier said than done.

Many military families are dealing with special needs children and face unknowns and uncertainty when relocating. Frequently, friends would ask whether I had everything we needed to help our children because of the frequent moves we were experiencing. As my son grew older, he was still very rambunctious, and a few teachers mentioned that he might need to be assessed to see whether he needed a prescription for Ritalin. I had to stand my ground concerning this, recognizing there was nothing wrong with my son being inquisitive and that he needed challenging instructions. He was bored, actually. I needed to be consistent and aware of how each of my children excelled. If you need help, get it. I asked questions, and if I needed more than one opinion, I would go get it. It was my responsibility to be aware of the needs of my child.

In the midst of it all, great things were still happening. My husband had now been selected for promotion to lieutenant colonel and was prepping for the next assignment.

Just as this joyous time came, tragedy struck again. My husband's mother passed away, devastating us once again. This loss carried a different amount of weight because she would not be at his promotion ceremony. Death has no respect of persons and comes when it is designated to do so. How were we to deal with a loss of this magnitude at such a critical time? We should have been celebrating a great accomplishment, and now, once again, here came grief.

Our children had not spent much time with their grandmother

because of the geographical distance caused by numerous military moves. I experienced waves of emotion at the mere thought that my own mother had passed away when I was twenty-seven years old and never had the chance to meet any of my children. My husband had always shared with us the foundational principles of his family, and his mother was a powerful and influential part of that foundation.

As we face life's battles, we can let them take us out, or we can let them fortify our minds and take us to the winner's circle.

The mind cannot comprehend the emotional state one will go through at the loss of a loved one, especially a parent. I had already experienced this early on in my life, and even though some time had passed, it was still not easy to deal with. We found it to be a day-by-day process. I don't believe anyone ever gets over it. You learn to accept it and to glean joy and peace from your memories. We worked hard to keep them alive, especially for our children.

As we face life's battles, we can let them take us out, or we can let them fortify our minds and take us to the winner's circle. When our service members are called into battle, they must possess the mindset that they will conquer the enemy. We don't wave a white flag in surrender or say, "Let's take a timeout to catch our breath." Life will continually present challenges. We must jump in with full force to win. That doesn't mean we will win every battle, but we do win the war. I have taken this same mental stand in my relationships, and I hold my ground to fight for them when we are going through a rough patch. Our love and support for one another help us push through our emotional weak place and build on that support to take another step into our destiny.

Triumphant Thinking

1. Make lemonade out of lemons. You may not find a job or start a career when you want to, but you have everything necessary to be successful inside of you.
2. Transparency brings liberation. Be true to yourself and acknowledge when you are not soaring with the eagles but are temporarily flying low. It's okay, and you will be okay.
3. Make memories with your family and focus on the good times while you have them. It's really all that counts.

SECTION 4
Success Initiatives

As we progressed through our twenty-two years of active duty, it occurred to me that four things had led to success, not just in the military, but in all walks of life. Those four things are (1) volunteer your time and talents, (2) be teachable, (3) invest in the future for yourself and others, and (4) prepare for shifts that come with time.

CHAPTER 13

Volunteering—It Makes a Difference (South Korea)

Up to this point, life had been exciting, challenging, and somewhat stressful, yet rewarding. It is always a good thing to stay alert in your subconscious and prepared for the unexpected. This is not to say we must live in fear or paranoia, but simply be in a place to handle anything out of the ordinary. That time came, and we had to experience it firsthand.

After a brief family discussion about our next assignment, my husband volunteered for a two-year accompanied assignment to South Korea. Our oldest daughter was going to start her freshman year in high school and definitely wanted to be in a place that would give her the chance to continue playing basketball at the next level and excel academically in preparation for college.

Our youngest child would be starting kindergarten, and our son would be going into the fourth grade. He would definitely need to stay focused on balancing his elevated performance in school and athletics. But what about me? Another move for two years—and not just across the country, but once again overseas, away from family, and the chance to work outside the home was much slimmer now.

I decided that each trial was another test of my fortitude. I didn't have a person or physical being whispering in my ear, reinforcing me, telling me I could handle anything and that this was another test to overcome. My faith was growing stronger with every instance and challenge. It was my choice how I would handle this move.

The proof I could handle it was replaying in my mind as I looked back over my life and recalled the outcome of each test and how I had come out on top. I truly believed the best was yet to come. I was living my life with great anticipation and expectation that if I lived a life centered on my faith, focused on helping others, loving my husband, and rearing good citizens (our children), then I could expect to live a life of abundance. I did not overlook the challenges and disappointments, but I realized it was my choice to decide how I would handle those issues.

There's a quote by Epictetus that says, "It's not what happens that determines the quality or quantity of your life, and the reason is that what happens—happens to about everyone." In other words, *"It's not what happens to you that counts but how you handle it."*

This mindset was possible because I surrounded myself with positive people. I began to read inspirational books and about people who were successful at living their best lives. This was a huge step in my personal growth, and I began to implement what I had learned with each move, and in each new relationship, I built. I know there will always be people I interact with who may bring a negative aura with them (e.g., the sandpaper people), but I have the freedom to exit their company. I don't have to entertain or accept what they bring. It's my choice.

The next big challenge came with shock and dismay. On September 11, 2001, while temporarily living in the Dragon Hill Lodge on the Yongsan Installation in South Korea, we were all preparing to turn in for the evening. We were watching Good Morning America when we witnessed two airplanes flying into the twin towers of the World Trade Center in New York City. I remember thinking this could not be happening. A burst of yellow and orange flames and plumes of black smoke started billowing from the building. It was unbelievable, and it felt as if my heart were about to stop beating.

"It's not what happens to you that counts but how you handle it."

An overwhelming, breathtaking emotional wave of grief rushed over me. Tears flooded my face as I beheld the unthinkable. We watched what millions of people around the world were witnessing. Our children were scared, upset, and unable to understand what was happening or why. Of course, that day is etched in my mind forever. The alerts began to sound, and it seemed chaotic for the rest of the evening, and for weeks to come, we were frozen in place in a hotel for about six weeks for security purposes. Our military members were on the highest alert, and every moment that they had trained for came to the forefront. Being thousands of miles from home and not knowing when we could move into our living quarters sent another emotional rollercoaster through my mind. But this was yet another call to duty, to rise up and be triumphant in the trenches.

Living in two adjoining rooms in a hotel for about six weeks was a task all its own. We eventually developed a daily schedule that had some sense to it, as we were able to get the children back into classes to get their minds focused on their classwork and not on whether or not they were safe living in South Korea.

Shortly thereafter, another turning point occurred for me, as I became involved with the Army Family Action Plan (AFAP) committee and volunteering with Army Family Team Building. Because of my interest in the wellbeing of people as a whole and my ability to communicate well with any culture or ethnicity, I came upon an opportunity that set my life on a course I never would have expected. The current challenges at that time focused on healthcare, educational benefits, and additional resources that would aid in the overall success of military members and their family members. We are now benefiting from the positive changes and outcomes that were discussed at that time.

The AFAP council played a huge role in the advancements of all branches of service pertaining to our healthcare benefits and extended educational options for the service member to gift their benefits to their spouse or children. The fact that family members can attend college in many states as residents and not suffer the out-of-state costs is the result of many years of spouses and committees fighting for these benefits. I was fortunate enough to travel back to the United States to participate in the National Conference for AFAP while stationed in South Korea.

This demonstrated how important my voice was and how to use it on behalf of all spouses and family members. Amazingly, most of these opportunities came to me as a volunteer.

The fact that I could not work in my academic field of study did not mean I could not use my voice for the greater good. Resilience became a way of life throughout the next few years and enabled me to shift with the moves and the anticipation for greater in both my husband's career and mine.

As I continued to build my skills and opened myself to possibilities outside of the box, I was selected to go to Atlanta, Georgia, for the Advanced Master Trainer course with Army Family Team Building. My communication skills, gained from my degree in broadcast journalism, were somehow making their way into play almost eighteen years later. As they say, timing is everything!

When you feel helpless and maybe even overlooked, you must look deep inside to see who you really are. What does your character say about you, and what do people see in you?

Positioning myself to fulfill my destiny was critical, and it was vital that I realize what I had been gifted to do and the impact I would have on the lives that I would touch. Many times, as spouses, we find ourselves in the valley of despair and pity because we have had to alter the plans or directions we thought our lives would take. Those plans may have been redirected, but I am writing to share my story to encourage others to get rid of that destructive way of thinking and realize your potential is as great as you want it to be, and it will take you as high as you will allow it to take you.

Thousands of books have been written on how to be successful and happy, but I found that the key to success and happiness lies within me. Happiness is normally driven by what happens to you, but how you deal with that produces either a positive or negative outcome.

> When you feel helpless and maybe even overlooked, you must look deep inside to see who you really are.

I believe wholeheartedly in the "law of reciprocity" and that the aura you give off draws like auras and likeminded people. When you want to gain wealth, you don't seek advice from those stuck in poverty. You ask those who are on the path in which you want to go. Over the years, I have observed that broken people surround themselves with other broken people and ask for their advice to get out of the trench they are in. Something just doesn't sound right with that approach.

Triumphant Thinking

1. Selflessness brings unexpected rewards.
2. What looks like it was designed to break you was designed to build you.
3. Say yes to new doors that may open even when you're not sure why you should walk through them.

CHAPTER 14

Be Teachable

As a master trainer for Army Family Team Building, I began to teach classes that helped spouses look through a different lens and find their untapped skills and abilities. This, thanks to my innate abilities, was a perfect platform for me to share the care and concern I had for people. Becoming an excellent communicator gave me a sense of great purpose. When I would see the light bulb come on in someone's thinking process after I clarified a point, I was even more certain I was doing what I was called to do. The more I was able to teach and provide briefings for the entire military arena at Yongsan, the more doors opened for me. One was a connection to a group called the Protestant Women of the Chapel.

> people will make their own assumptions about you no matter what you do.

This group provided my spiritual support and a time of reflection that also met many other needs for spouses who felt abandonment, despair, or marital distress. Many of the spouses I worked with were avoiding dealing with their personal challenges with others, fearing judgment or embarrassment. I encouraged the spouses to evaluate where they were and recognize that this was the time to stretch past their feelings and ask for help. Being a preacher's kid and living in a fishbowl, I learned early on that *people will make their own assumptions about you no matter what you do.* So you may as well live your most authentic life.

There was a weekend retreat held for the entire South Korea

peninsula for women called Faith Lift. About three hundred women attended, and the keynote speaker was brought in from the United States to share an encouraging message of hope. I had the privilege to be assigned as the adjutant (or assistant) for that speaker. When we met, our interaction was subtle yet interesting. As most of my friends know, I am a jovial, happy-go-lucky individual and very optimistic. As the adjutant for the keynote speaker, I was responsible for meeting her for lunch, making sure all her needs were taken care of, and assisting with the setup and preparation for her presentation. I didn't know I was about to experience a wakeup call.

I met the speaker for lunch in a nice, cozy cafe in the hotel. I was my usual perky self. When we sat down at the table, the conversation started with this statement from the speaker: "You need to quiet your spirit down. It's too busy." I was stunned and somewhat taken aback. What exactly did that mean? She never really explained it, but went on to tell me what she needed for her presentation and provided a timeline for the event. As graciously as I could, I smiled and listened for the details, and ate my food quietly. After lunch, we headed over to the venue to make sure everything was set up to her satisfaction.

That statement changed my view of myself, and I sought a deeper understanding to make sure I was not fooling myself. Who was I, and who was I created to be? What about me caused that reaction? Then the reality hit me. Not everyone is happy, and not everyone is at peace with who they are, and my mere being may not agree with their perceptions. I was just fine and now even more equipped to use my influence, because I had been given a new awareness of the power that resided in me, to live victoriously in every situation. Living *triumphantly in the trenches.*

I didn't change who I was, but I gained a new awareness. I've had the opportunity to interact with many personalities throughout my lifetime, maturing and applying what I've gained from each experience. It has really paid off. I had to move past the surface of my emotional state to get to the deeper internal revelation of who I am and how my life's experiences have transformed me into the individual I have become. I was not upset. Neither do I hold any ill feelings toward the speaker, but actually, I was filled with gratitude, because her words pushed me to another level, helping me identify just how strong I was as a woman and the privilege I had to affect thousands of lives.

Shortly after the retreat, I was selected to travel to Florida to represent the Protestant Women of the Chapel as the chaplain for our group. It was yet another experience to solidify my purpose and increase my faith, to continue being who I was created to be, and to be a powerful influence in every life I touched.

What does it mean to be a military spouse? Being a military spouse is a category all to itself. It requires the ability to multitask, to create a safe atmosphere and home wherever that may be, to face emergencies that may arise while your spouse is deployed or not available to assist, and to do it with grace and poise—a tall order to say the least. We may make it look easy, and for some, it may appear glamorous, but the truth is that it is highly stressful, lonely, difficult, and sometimes disappointing. Being honest and facing the reality that we live in is the only way we can survive. *We win some battles and lose some, but we are never down for the count.* We develop internal fortitude as we face our daily challenges, schedules, and the unexpected. Let us not overlook the issues that our spouses are faced with every day. The next major event that occurred became an international story and directly affected my husband.

On a normal workday, as my husband was driving in, he received a call from one of his colleagues who informed him that their boss (an army colonel) had just been taken into custody by the Central Intelligence Division and military police. As he approached the building where he worked, he saw yellow investigation tape surrounding the building and men in uniforms with weapons and civilians with badges. He was informed that his superiors, both military and civilian, had been arrested for embezzlement and other unethical activities. This was a full-blown "sting" operation and investigation into illegal activity over several years. A real shock, as you can imagine. My husband was suddenly the director of contracting while maintaining his own position as chief of contract operations.

> We win some battles and lose some, but we are never down for the count.

The organization had to continue providing contracting support to all the units on the peninsula while going through a very high-profile case. This crisis forced my husband to work even more hours, and he found himself exhausted in the evenings. Eventually, the excessive work hours and stress took their toll and affected his health. Nevertheless, he survived and was *triumphant in the trenches.*

Often, we don't realize the impact of the stress our service members endure and how it affects their families and their marriages. Military spouses often endure the stresses of their military members and experience the consequences too. Sayings such as "Suck it up buttercup" or "Drive on" pressure the service member to keep pushing, even when they need help, and should step back to assess how situations have affected them personally.

> If you need help, it's there. Take advantage of the provisions.

For years, these resources were not available, but they are now and quite extensive and available to the entire family to aid them in navigating their personal struggles as a family. Counseling services for each member can be obtained. There are special sessions for children, teaching them to help them cope with loss, fear, and mental anguish. The Department of Veterans Affairs has increased its number of employees, programs, and benefits to provide for a solid life for those who are currently serving or have served our country. *If you need help, it's there. Take advantage of the provisions.*

Triumphant Thinking

1. It's your choice how you handle what happens to you. Always go high.
2. Criticism is actually a prop to take you to the next level. Use it and keep it moving.
3. Life has a tendency to course correct; accept it, it is working for your good.

CHAPTER 15

Invest in the Future

During this season, my husband's shift into overdrive didn't seem to affect our home negatively. Our children were flourishing. Our oldest daughter was still excelling in her academic endeavors, as a 4.0 student with a new declaration to attend Stanford University in Palo Alto, California. As a freshman starting on the varsity basketball team, she had recently received the MVP award during a tournament held in Guam.

Our son, now in fifth grade, was enjoying a stint of acting in a children's educational series. We did not know this was a precursor of his future, as he is now an acclaimed actor with a graduate degree in acting (masters of fine arts) from the California Institute of the Arts. Life was not easy for him during his adolescent years, as he was highly intelligent and very curious. His ability to focus was challenged, and school counselors once again suggested he needed Ritalin to get him through his school days. Even though this may be necessary for some children, I did not agree and chose not to engage. My son was bored and lacking the challenges needed to assist him as he was excelling at a higher level. He was also tested and found to be gifted and talented, so there was a definite disconnect. My homeschooling increased to help offset what we were facing.

If your child needs extra support or assistance, get involved, and do your own research. I had to look beyond the typical diagnosis to make sure I was aiding my son and not allowing a system to hurt him.

Our little four-year-old kindergartner was enjoying competing in gymnastics under the tutelage of South Korean Olympic coach Mr. Pak. She traveled throughout the peninsula and was exposed to the best and most elite gyms while working out with the top Korean gymnasts. Her ability to do back handsprings, aerials, balance beam, and parallel bars at this age was amazing. Modeling on runways at major fashion shows was also a joy in which she delighted.

This was a very busy time for our household. As I found, I had a gift for rearing my own children, I found that I had a love for assisting others with theirs as well, and I seemed to be a magnet to youths of all ages.

Soon after joining the women's group and kicking off a marriage-enrichment class for the chapel, I realized that the children lacked involvement in the service, and a youth chorale group was created. Hailing from a musical family and having two children that were gifted with instruments, I jumped in, and another opportunity became one with great reward. The youth chorale grew to more than fifty youths, and we sang at local events in the area as well. I was busier than I had ever been, and all this was volunteer work. So much invested, and at the end of it all, my oldest daughter and I received the Volunteer of the Year awards from the Eighth US Army. Wow! How fulfilled were our lives as we gave out to others in need, building others up and encouraging them to know that they too could have what we had: love, focus, and selflessness. This is what being triumphant looks like, from my perspective.

> Sharing these particular events brings a pattern to light: when we focus and give our time to causes outside ourselves, we grow as individuals.

Sharing these particular events brings a pattern to light: when we focus and give our time to causes outside ourselves, we grow as individuals. Our overall ability to succeed when faced with personal struggles and disappointments came from reflecting on the positives and the victories we experienced in the past. There is a cost to success. Maybe as you are reading my story, you are thinking, Is this really true? How could there be this much positive when there are so many negatives? It is true. This is how I have lived my entire life. It's a choice.

For some, the stories and accomplishments I have shared may not mean much, but because we have given so much of ourselves and seen such positive results, we had to celebrate each moment—because the next challenge was right around the corner. Over the years, many people have asked me how we experienced so much success. Maintaining our stick-to-itiveness has been a huge component, helping us stay focused as we've moved toward our destiny.

> *Sacrifice is a part of life. It's supposed to
> be. It's not something to regret.
> It's something to aspire to.*
> —Mitch Albom

What does success truly look like for you? It looks different for everyone, and the cost to achieve it also varies. I had to assess what I was willing to give up to achieve it. Sometimes I sacrificed my money, my time, my resources, my skills, and my abilities to assist others. The validation I received by giving to others and knowing I helped improve the lives of many has been worth it all. One of the principles I live by is this: *be the change that I want to see*. I know that my purpose is greater than I could have ever imagined, and success really can't be summed up in a few words. I am determined to accomplish whatever I set my mind to, and that will define success in whatever form that takes.

Once I discovered my purpose, the roadmap took on a whole new shape, and the real fight began. Once I decided that I was going to pursue my dream no matter what, my mindset shifted to a place of fierceness. Keeping my focus helped me deal with doubt, disappointment, unexpected delays, complacency, rejection, and confusion. The fear of being successful can be just as daunting as the fear of failure.

Sacrifice for anything worthy takes on a new look when you are steadfast in your commitment to achieving your goals. Once I admitted that I was the only person standing in the way of my success, I could then eliminate some of the obstacles. I would often share with my children that people will always be a variable in how you obtain your success; some will be your greatest cheerleaders, and others will be your greatest critics. I have always encouraged my children to align themselves with what they believed to be the truth about themselves, using it as a weapon to fight off naysayers. Whatever I think about myself is what I present to others. One of the many principles I instilled in my children was to stay true to yourself and allow the process to get you where you are trying to go.

Staying the course is paramount, recognizing that sacrifice comes in many different forms. Sometimes it is friendships and the freedom to do what may not be convenient at the time. It takes discipline and accountability. *Procrastination and excuses are huge enemies of progress.* I often had to make a timeline to keep me on track and make steady progress.

Remember, timing is everything. When you have a vision, a call, or destiny in your purview, putting off for tomorrow what you need to accomplish today could halt your momentum. As I have continued to move along life's journey towards achieving my dreams, revisiting and reassessing my goals has become very important. Hard work pays off. Recognizing small incremental victories along the way has kept my adrenaline high and provided a boost of encouragement to continue with the same or greater tenacity.

> *Without commitment, you'll never get started.*
> *Without consistency, you'll never succeed.*
> —Denzel Washington

So, after enjoying some small victories and successes and surviving the storm with my husband's job, another one hit. The pollution in Korea at that time was ranked third in the world, and it had now affected my husband's voice. He had basically lost it. He was now walking around with a box designed to amplify his voice so he could be heard. We soon relocated back to the United States, and within a few months, his voice returned. Several years of vocal therapy were required to repair the damage to his vocal cords and to teach them to use his voice in a healthy manner to avoid a setback.

> Procrastination and excuses are huge enemies of progress.

Before leaving Yongsan, we had been approached several times by the post chaplain about us conducting marriage classes. Each time, my husband declined, saying it wasn't our "area of expertise." The chaplain was persistent, and after the third request, another destiny moment was birthed. Our commitment to one another, our strong communication skills, and the results in our own relationship were evidence enough to gain the trust of many couples.

Thus, our next unexpected assignment began. It was without a doubt divine intervention that set our paths in this direction. This is the catalyst that eventually guided us to create a nonprofit marriage-enrichment ministry. It led to my husband writing a book on marriage as well. Talk about strategic placement – right place, right time. That is exactly what our tour in Korea provided. It was clearly in preparation for the next chapter of our lives.

Triumphant Thinking

1. Establish strong principles early to maintain strong character later.
2. Be your authentic self. Don't confuse who you want to be with who you are.
3. Allow your natural gifts and talents to position you for your next level assignment.

CHAPTER 16

The Shift

Hello, sunny Southern California! We were thrilled to finally be stationed in San Diego. I was finally going to get to know my two older sisters that were also living in California. My sisters moved to Sacramento shortly after they graduated from high school (in the 70s) to live with my oldest sister (now deceased). We had tried for over twenty years to get stationed there, and now we had finally made it. We were excited and ready for the next chapter.

My husband was about to embark upon a unique assignment as where he would be the only army soldier assigned to a joint organization with sailors, airmen, and marines at the Space and Naval Warfare Systems Command (SPAWAR) in San Diego. Looking back, it was the start of something great and the end of a wonderful military career.

This was a transitional period for our whole family, as our oldest daughter was in her junior year of high school, our son was beginning sixth school, and our youngest daughter was entering first grade. I believe this was the biggest transition for our children, especially our oldest daughter, because it was at this time she would start to look at colleges and determining exactly what she wanted to do in her future.

The adjustment was a bit of a struggle, as many of you know, from personal experience or from someone you may know, how mean and unwelcoming some kids can be. Trying to fit into a new school scene with preexisting girl cliques was not fun. Although she was a starter on the varsity team, basketball was not without challenges and disappointments. So she opted to forego her senior year of playing the game and focused 100 percent on her academics as she prepared to apply to college. It was well worth the effort, as she was accepted by her top two picks (Stanford and Harvard).

The tides began to turn for my son, as he was finding his way and so was I. Most days, it was pretty chaotic getting out of the house, as there was always a challenge with looking for shoes, a backpack, homework, or a jacket. It seemed that we were at odds just getting to the car, and even though I would say, "I love you," as he exited at the drop off point, I'm sure he was questioning it because of our routine debates. An incident one morning, as we prepared to leave the house for school, changed both of our lives as mother and son. This particular morning, just as we had done so many times before, we were standing at the front door about to leave, and I was yelling and trying to move as expeditiously as possible so that my son and youngest daughter would not be late for school. Suddenly, I heard a still small voice. It was very clear and distinct. "Do I speak to you that way?"

I looked around to see if someone had walked up to the front door, and then I looked back at my son, who was standing with glassy eyes and a somewhat frustrated wrinkle across his forehead. My daughter had already gone to the car, and there was no one else around. I didn't address this at that moment, but a quiet calm came over me as I drove to the school.

After I returned home, I sat quietly in meditation, trying to decipher what had just happened. As tears began to flow down my cheeks, I realized that the chaos and acting out by our son was being fueled by me. He knew he could not respond or lash out at me, but when he got to school, he was so frustrated, he had to do something to release his anger and probably his disappointment as well. Hence, the busyness, distractions, and lack of ability to stay focused even though he was brilliant.

> Live every day as a reflection of what you speak about. Let self-control and discipline be habits of your character.

When he returned home, I decided to ask for forgiveness. I knew I had not really been listening to him or giving him respect as a human by yelling and rushing him out of the house each morning. From that moment, our relationship shifted into something wonderful.

Live every day as a reflection of what you speak about. Let self-control and discipline be habits of your character.

Our son made the adjustment really well to middle school and made some good friends who had similar backgrounds and demeanors. He soon discovered his ability to speak publically and won a $1,500 college scholarship at a regional optimist oratorical competition. As I mentioned earlier, he is currently a professional actor, and winning this oratorical contest proved to be a stepping-stone towards his future. Public speaking came natural to him, and it helped channel his high energy and passions.

Our youngest daughter was fitting in well at her elementary school and wanted to hang out more with her friends, so I enrolled her in the afterschool program. This was when we discovered that not only did our son have a gift in public speaking and acting, but so did our daughter.

The afterschool program provided an array of opportunities in singing, acting, community service, and academic growth. As a parent of three gifted children, I had to constantly read and familiarize myself with current events and computer knowledge, as they were being required more and more to create presentations, write papers, and present oneself in public arenas. Taking advantage of the resources on the installations was an added bonus. The libraries, youth programs, and workshops kept them connected with the lifestyle they were accustomed to as they learned to blend into the civilian community.

My journalism skills and my husband's leadership positions and excellent writing ability were having a major impact on our children as well. It was if he transferred his skills and his analytical thinking style to them, while my creative style broadened their scope. Each of them developed a keen insight and understanding of the English language and how to write far above their grade levels. This, surely, has been one of the results of my sacrifice to stay at home with them for as long as I did to cultivate their academic foundation.

How do you rear gifted children and keep them balanced, humbled, and encouraged to excel at the same time? Not to mention, let them be kids and have fun too. My husband and I felt strongly that you must live the example before them, because we were their first role models. This mindset would definitely come into play in a huge way later. Allowing our children to express themselves in a positive way and teaching them the household boundaries ensured a safe place for them to learn, develop, make mistakes, and try again.

In order to produce a functional family, we felt it was important to have fun with our children and build lifelong positive memories such as taking vacations (not expensive ones), playing basketball together, going to the movies, playing games at home, writing and producing songs, having dinner together, praying together, etc. In addition, we created a few traditions. For example, each person opened one present on Christmas Eve. *The key is not necessarily the activities, but more so the time doing them together.*

My husband and I didn't have all the answers, but we were committed to being present and involved with our children. We created an environment that allowed them to engage in activities that were of interest to them and provided the chance to experience a variety of things so they would never feel limited in what they could achieve. This was a stretch for me, as I had put my dreams on hold to nurture theirs.

> The key is not necessarily the activities, but more so the time doing them together.

There is a thin line that one must always be aware of as you enter this season of your life. It can be deceiving and easy to become resentful or bitter if you allow it to take you over. Often, it looks as though everyone else is moving forward and achieving their goals while you seem to be in a support role and neglecting your own goals. Deal with it for what it is—temporary, and maybe, just maybe, a blessing in disguise. I often had to reassess my position and make decisions I felt were best at the time for the family. It was not always easy, but the choices always paid off in the end.

Success comes in a steady pace through the bends and winding curves of everyday life.

Be advised, there was a lot of work and much sacrifice during this time. We were often exhausted trying to keep up with a busy schedule of events and maintaining a solid balance at home. Difficult choices had to be made, and it was not always easy. It was beyond our own capacity to see the results that would come from the early investment in our children. The rewards that we have received far outweigh the hurried, sometimes chaotic lifestyle at the time.

By this time in my life, I had come to realize that in the midst of good times, there normally comes a time of opposition, more challenges, and sometimes heartbreak. As in the past, the next tragedy occurred. My father passed away.

> Success comes in a steady pace through the bends and winding curves of everyday life.

With each death that I had to face, I seemed to handle it in a different way. Sometimes, I didn't know how it affected me until years later. It depended on the depth of the relationship and what my core beliefs and support systems looked like at that time. Not having any regrets about what I should have done helped my subconscious mind. If we have not dealt with a problem within our relationship when someone passes away, that problem tends to haunt us or maybe even take us on a guilt trip. Remembering the stages of grief, I learned about earlier and understanding what stage I was in helped me to cope and get through it.

I was actually a daddy's girl until I turned fourteen years old and all my siblings had moved on. The change that took place was like night and day from then on. My dad was laying down the law of the land, and I was not having any of it. One day, I realized it was just his way of showing me that he loved me and wanted the best for me. In the midst of my sadness, I turned to my faith and celebrated memories of many joyful and productive days with my dad. I hold one memory dear in particular. I was in the seventh grade, and my dad took me out of school to go hunting with him. He bred greyhounds and was an avid hunter, and I had begged for years to go, but he always told me I was too young. That was the first time I learned how to shoot a shotgun, and I was actually really good at it.

Another strong memory is how my father took a liking to my husband before we were married. I recall the two of them in deep conversations about life, the ministry, and integrity. He even took him hunting. They gave me peace and resolve that all was well.

Special memories like these gave me the needed strength once again to power through what could have been a very depressing time. As each of my loved ones who had passed away brought a different stint of grief, I somehow grew stronger in my immediate relationships. I learned to live in the present and to invest in the time we shared and created very special memories.

My father was a giant of a man in character and heart. As a preacher, pastor, and bishop within our denomination, his huge spirit of giving, benevolence, empowerment, and quest for what is right left a void not only in the lives of his biological children, but in the community at large.

During my childhood, my father was always jovial and well respected throughout the city. Although he was a stern disciplinarian and very strict in raising my siblings and me, he was a man of great integrity and professionalism. He stood tall in the eyes of the many who benefitted from his mentorship and financial assistance. We did not have much, but my father always found a way to help those in need and less fortunate than we were. His acts of charity and genuine concern for others are foundational blocks that greatly influenced our family values.

Planning is paramount in preparation for separation or retirement.

Back in those days, a man's word was considered his bond and could be trusted no matter what. The drive to be better educated than his father and mother and to live a life worth noting established a strong constitution within me to do the same. My husband possesses those same character traits and has also established them for our children. It's never too late to create a legacy that will take the next generation to a better place than they are now.

I realize that not everyone has good memories of their childhood and that there is many hurting, disappointed people living with resentment. I experienced some of those emotions at various times, but I chose to move past them. I didn't want to give more power to those who had hurt or disappointed me by holding on to the pain.

The time had come, and the preparation for our transition out of the military into the civilian sector was nearer than we thought. *Planning is paramount in preparation for separation or retirement.* There are several steps that should start at least two years out from the final date. In most cases, and depending on your financial situation, if you haven't saved and invested for separation or retirement, you will need to start years earlier to be in a position to make difficult decisions more bearable. Having a targeted resume for a specific job and knowing how to prepare for the interviewing process are also important considerations to transition to the civilian workforce. Take the time to attend all available transition readiness courses in whichever branch of service you are in. It will be the catalyst for success as you transition or retire.

For the next three years, my husband worked diligently in his last assignment at SPAWAR and simultaneously prepared for life after the military. We had a beautiful retirement ceremony that brought many of our family and friends together from near and far. We moved forward with great expectations for the next season of our lives.

Triumphant Thinking

1. Have a solid exit plan for retirement, or you may have to come out of it later.
2. Learn the strengths of your children's personalities so you can live more harmoniously.
3. Some parenting methods may seem harsh to your children at the time, but no concern at all would be unproductive in the end.

SECTION 5
Strategic Alignment

In these days and times, positioning yourself for the right opportunity begins with (1) Networking, and recognizing your season in (2) Leadership vs. Servanthood will help you rise out of despair when you need to implement (3) The Next Game Plan, when yours have been (4) Delayed, but not Denied, and remain flexible about (5) Sacrificing, because That's What We Do. We've been created for a great purpose.

CHAPTER 17

Networking

Networking is not just a cliché. It does work.

While attending a scholarship awards dinner, I met someone who was working for the Marine and Family Programs on Camp Pendleton, and as we spoke, we realized my experiences as an army spouse and my years of volunteering with military families and programs made me a good fit for some new programs being created. Some months later, I followed up; the positions were now open, and I applied. All the years of staying connected to the various installations through volunteering and continuously building my resume were paying off.

> It became apparent that networking and timing were key components of success.

As a military spouse, I was constantly in a state of flux, being displaced and having to relocate because of the change in duty stations. I found out later that following up with unemployment within each state could have benefited me, as I would have received compensation for my displacement. I also checked in with the installation's Community Services programs to find out what other benefits I had as a spouse.

I accepted a position with Family Team Building as a Family Readiness Advisor. It was a newly created position that allowed me to become certified in many areas ranging from personality assessments, unit trainings, deployments, and command briefs. Everything I had been trained in, volunteered for, and learned over the past eighteen years had come full circle, and now I was actually getting paid for what I loved to do. *It became apparent that networking and timing were key components of success.*

As a spouse who had struggled with finding a job or defining my career path, I was encouraged to know that there was a program designed just for spouses to assist with that. I tapped into the Family Member Employment Assistance Program on my installation. It is specifically designed to help spouses in career identification, career strategies, resume assistance, interviewing, and salary negotiation. I also discovered that most installations have an educational center as well that can help with the search for four-year colleges, two-year institutions, and even certification programs. The answer was only as far away as seeking the available resources.

Preparation has been the key to achieving my goals. While I was waiting to acquire a paid job or career, I made certain to function as if I already had it. I had basic business cards printed up with my information and kept updated resumes with me. I attended every networking event, job search event, career fair, and events hosted to provide me with access to employers, recruiters, or headhunters. I created my thirty-second "elevator speech" and prepared to share my worth and value at an instant.

Being prepared when the opportunity presented itself was half of the battle. There is nothing more tragic than meeting the one person who can offer you the job or change the direction of your career and not be prepared to present. I took advantage of programs and resources on each installation that was specifically designed to help me be successful and set me on a path to achieving my life's goals.

If I had resigned myself to stay at home and become complacent about my situation, or had I been satisfied only with volunteering, I would have never ventured out to an event that provided me with the life-changing opportunities I am still benefiting from today. I wanted more, the time had come, and I was able to capitalize on it.

For the next four years, I experienced some of the greatest accomplishments in my career, as I had the opportunity to present at Quantico Marine Corps Base to the new incoming commanders and spouses on the effectiveness of one of the programs that would benefit their commands. Camp Pendleton was recognized as one of the leaders in the success of how these new programs were being rolled out and received. This success was due largely to the great team of advisors we had in Family Team Building.

Being an innovative person, I was always seeking out programs that would benefit our service members and their families. As a certified Prevention Relationship Enhancement Program (PREP) instructor, which deals with relationships, along with the fact that my husband and I had founded a nonprofit marriage-enrichment organization, opened the door for us to facilitate Dr. Gary Chapman's The Five Love Languages workshop. After attending a marriage retreat in Arizona that featured Dr. Chapman as the keynote speaker, I helped orchestrate his visit to Camp Pendleton for a reception and dinner session with a local faith-based church. Fifty local military couples were selected to attend the event and enjoy a private session during the dinner with Dr. Chapman. What an awesome experience and morale booster for our couples. The Five Love Languages workshop was very well received throughout most branches of the military. I had the distinguished honor to present it in Washington, D.C., for the Sergeant Majors and Spouses conference.

It doesn't matter how long you have been married; you are forever learning, changing, and growing. There are versions of The Five Love Languages for all family members and one designed for the military in particular.

The knowledge and wisdom I have gained over the years as a military spouse had come through many hours of counseling, researching, studying, and developing my skills and abilities. The passion that I have for helping others always manifested itself wherever I would go. I have found that people are just people wanting to be respected, loved, and validated. Military rank or status never impeded my ability to assist anyone in need of my help.

The worthwhile relationships I have built through the years, reflects humanity at its best.

During the time I was a Family Readiness Advisor, I had the responsibility of conveying the importance of reaching members that had endured some negative experiences in the military and were struggling to acclimate. That meant reaching the spouse, children, and parents, which comprised the extended support system for the service member. In the trenches, you get dirty, trampled on, overlooked, and sometimes abused. I may not have received many pats on the back while serving in this role, but the rewards I received after seeing how my assistance had a major impact was priceless.

Living triumphantly in the trenches is a lifestyle, not just a statement.

My light has shone the brightest in darkness, and that is why it takes a special person to serve in the military and, even more so, to be a spouse. It is not for the faint of heart.

Networking has opened doors I would have never walked through on my own. Being friendly, approachable, and genuinely interested in people draws people from all walks of life, countries, ethnicities, and backgrounds. I am an international traveler, and I would say a sort of "bootleg" ambassador. It's not an official position, but I take it to heart. This attitude was strengthened and developed throughout the years my husband served on active duty, which has taken us before ambassadors and royalty around the world. The saying "It's not just what you know but who you know" is absolutely true.

My father taught us that it was more valuable to have a good name than all of the riches in this world. He would say, "Your good name gives you access to people, places, and things that your money cannot buy." He also taught me that my word is my bond. If I tell you that you can count on me, you can. Do not judge a person before you get to know them. They may have to save your life one day. *Living triumphantly in the trenches is a lifestyle, not just a statement.*

With every certification I received as a Family Readiness Advisor, I assessed the impact that it would have and the influence I was given to help better the lives of our service members and families. As with any job, the time came for changes in personnel and programs. I had given my best as an advisor in this capacity, and now it was time to shift again.

With each new opportunity, I faced obstacles and challenges. I understand now that when achieving great feats and accomplishments, it comes with the territory. The change for me was necessary to grow and develop new skills and abilities as I sharpened the ones I already had. I welcomed the next level that tested me to live triumphantly in the trenches.

Triumphant Thinking

1. Proper positioning prepares for opportunity.
2. Preparation positions you for success.
3. Taking action accesses the open door.

CHAPTER 18

Leadership vs. Servanthood

After a twenty-two year career, my husband retired from the army in 2006. He was offered a position with a highly reputable major defense contractor in San Diego, working on a multi-billion-dollar joint program led by the navy. Things seemed to be moving in the right direction, and this was a good move, since he could continue to commute using the train into the city and be minutes from his job.

Things went well for three years and then suddenly went south. My husband was notified that he was being laid off due to program budget cuts. This came as a surprise and a disappointment as he was the most senior qualified person in his division. Nevertheless, he took it all in stride. He immediately starting job hunting and spent an incredible amount of hours every day and night searching and applying for jobs. He kept a log of all the jobs he applied for and stopped counting after number three hundred. Recruiters would always tell him that, with his credentials, he should be getting offers frequently. But he wasn't. We had no idea that it would be four years later before he signed another employment contract, with a company in the Middle East. That was a real eye-opener for both of us. I would have to write another book to cover every emotional, financial, and mental process we both maneuvered through during this time.

During the four years my husband was unemployed, we struggled financially because of the loss of his income. Although I was working now, we had to now micromanage our money. We understand what it means to live paycheck to paycheck. He would always say, "We may not have a lot of money, but we have never missed a meal or a bill." The cost of living in Southern California is one of the highest in the United States. This was a tough experience that I share with anyone preparing for retirement or transition from the military. Take it seriously, and have a backup plan. *You may have a stellar military career, be held in high regard, and even hold a high rank, but that does not mean you will step into the same situation in the civilian sector.*

This crisis fueled my passion even more, as I taught classes at Camp Pendleton encouraging military members to make sure they seriously thought about options as well as employment and where they would live as they got closer to transitioning from the military.

While my husband was dealing with the situation in his own way and trying to make the best of this difficult period, he never seemed to let it get him down. He was frustrated, yes, but never depressed. We both believed that when one door closes, God is opening another one. And boy did He. One benefit during this four-year layoff was that my husband was able to spend more quality time with our youngest daughter, who was in high school. He became affectionately known as "Mr. Taxi."

Like many women I have spoken to that were facing these same circumstances, I wanted security. Military life provides an unparalleled amount of job security for the service member and his or her family. The benefits and on-time salary can lull you into an alternate world where you don't have to worry about medical bills, dental bills, utility bills, or rent/mortgage (if you live on post/base). Looking back at the period, my demeanor was, I'm okay if he is okay. Was I concerned more than a little? Absolutely!

> You may have a stellar military career, be held in high regard, and even hold a high rank, but that does not mean you will step into the same situation in the civilian sector.

As we tried to figure out how we would live in Southern California with its high cost of living, the stress meter was swiftly moving to the right. At first, it didn't seem as though it was going to be an issue, since I was working and we had my husband's retirement income, but after a few months of applying for positions and coming up empty, the intensity of the situation began to grow.

On top of this, our son was about to graduate from high school. He had applied to several colleges and universities, and had not heard back from any of them. What was going on? He was a stellar student and athlete, the captain of the basketball team, lead actor for the theater department, and the school sports commissioner. But there was another plan for his life.

One of my friends who spoke at a weekend event recommended that my son and husband contact a university about an hour north of our home and go up for an interview and a tour. That same week, he received acceptance to Vanguard University to attend beginning in the fall of that year and received scholarships for academics and theater. He also had the opportunity to play on the varsity basketball team. Not only did we fight through our own trenches, but we survived those of our children as well.

We had been teaching our children the same principles we were living by, and to give credit to our son, his disposition through the whole process was very calm. He was contented to attend a community college and live at home while preparing to attend a four-year school. This was living triumphantly as a teenager and was a considerable shift from his former teenage years.

While looking for employment, my husband volunteered his time working for our faith affiliation and assisting the pastor. This commitment became very time consuming, but I feel it was exactly what he needed during his daily job hunt. I have read many different quotes that state, "To be a good leader, you must first be a good follower." I believe that in this season of my husband's life, he shifted from being a leader in a specific area to being more of a follower.

The months carried over into years, and now, the question arose as to whether he needed to go back to school. Although we had a great relationship and had learned to support one another in whatever season of life we were in, this was definitely new territory. A doctoral program is very time consuming and equivalent to no other academic challenge.

A few years before this, we had founded a nonprofit marriage-enrichment ministry designed to help couples build strong marriages with communication tools, and my husband had written a book providing additional insights called, *It's OK to Have an Affair (with Your Spouse)*. Yes, a unique title that certainly grabs your attention. The book contains thirty-two pearls of wisdom to help build a strong bond and relationship. We were literally living out the pearls every day. For example, "Pearl #14: Stress is inevitable in marriage. Prepare for it." "Pearl #22: Don't stretch yourself too thin, too long. It will only stress you out, which will make you tired, irritable, and difficult to get along with." We weren't difficult to deal with, but the typical attacks that come along with any relationship were intensifying, waiting to see if we could survive the trench.

Just because you have a strong marriage that is built on strong principles does not mean you will not face challenges and have to work through your differences.

Helping other couples and being honest and addressing those challenges upfront gave us a better chance of resolution. We drew closer and became even stronger as we faced the next situation to arise.

While teaching the transition workshops, I covered the various programs that the military offers, such as counseling and marriage retreats through the chaplains, as well as many relationship workshops geared toward the single service member. The significance of these programs is invaluable based on the high incidence of divorce and relationship issues in the military.

Marriage is already something you have to work at consistently. You must constantly build, strengthen, and relook to keep it healthy and functioning properly. When you consider the many challenges associated with military life, relationships can take on a whole new look. As many military spouses had to deal with the long hours, in addition to the deployments, other issues come into play. There are many accounts of alcohol or drug abuse, financial problems, infidelity, and emotional/psychological challenges due to deployments and disappointments. Many service members find it difficult to talk about what they are going through and don't seek help until they are suffering side effects from medications they are taking to cope with their problems.

> Just because you have a strong marriage that is built on strong principles does not mean you will not face challenges and have to work through your differences.

Studies have been done for decades on how men communicate

differently than women. Men do not always find it easy to communicate what they are going through, as they are trained from a young age to suck it up and drive on. My husband and I have developed a strong and open line of communication over the years, but it has taken that time to do so.

While on active duty, there were many situations that my husband faced that he either couldn't or didn't share with me. This could have caused problems because of the loss of trust or the appearance he was hiding something. Sometimes he just seemed distant. But after gaining knowledge from the various classes I was teaching and participating in workshops designed to help families members communicate effectively, it was easier to implement what I had learned and deal with the situations. Understanding the various stages of separation was one of many key factors that helped me create a balance in our home in between deployments.

According to the Marines Corps Family Team Building workshop material I taught, there are seven stages of the emotional cycle of deployment that I believe is also applicable to any type of separation for an extended period of time.

(Marine Corps Family Team Building) Under the 7 stages of the cycles of Emotional Deployment

The Seven Stages of the Emotional Cycle of Deployment

Stage 1: Anticipation of departure
Stage 2: Detachment and withdrawal
Stage 3: Emotional disorder
Stage 4: Recovery and stabilization
Stage 5: Anticipation of return
Stage 6: Return adjustment and renegotiation
Stage 7: Reintegration and stabilization

In the stages of separation, I found that stage 2, detachment and withdrawal, was one of the most difficult to work through. Although it may seem odd that a couple would be detached when approaching a deployment, by being irritable and confrontational, it was fairly common. Sometimes it is easier to feel mad than it is to accept the reality of their leaving. However, this anger results in guilt and anxiety once the spouse is actually deployed. You start thinking about how you would feel if something tragic happened after departing on a bad note.

Each stage brings about change that can be good for some and not so good for others. Once a spouse has actually deployed, there is a period of disorganization and feeling out of control. You try to get some sense of what you're feeling, and this could be depression or helplessness. When my husband was unemployed for almost four years, I was accustomed to him being home and having a sense of security and familiarity in his comings and goings, but when he accepted a job overseas, although I had agreed to it, I later felt abandoned and almost helpless. Because of my inclination to handle things no matter what, I didn't stay in that stage very long, because I couldn't afford to. The responsibility of carrying on and getting our youngest daughter ready for college became my focus at that time. I moved right into stage 4: "recovery and stabilization," and became confident once again that I was fully able to handle anything that came my way.

In this stage, one becomes very comfortable with their routine. You are independent and make necessary decisions without a lot of dialogue and banter about the outcome. For some women, this is empowering, motivating, and a huge confidence builder, but for others, it can seem daunting, overwhelming, and unfair. Depending on your perspective and your upbringing, the impact can be crucial.

Just as we progressed to this stage in the process, I found it was also challenging reverting to our prior state when my husband returned during his personal time off. The information on the cycles of deployment can be found online at MilitaryOneSource.com and at local installations, usually through the Family Team Building services. What worked for me was being open-minded, understanding, patient, and, most of all, loving.

Situations in life come to help us accomplish many different things;

sometimes, we aren't really sure what they are at that time. I really can't say to someone who has lost their job, "I know how you feel," because although I have left jobs because of our moves, I have never received a "pink slip" (employment termination notice). What I can say is that I know many people who have and have seen the devastation, uncertainty, and impact to their self-confidence. If the individual is the primary income earner, as my husband was, it can be even more devastating. The longer it takes for them to become employed again, the more difficult it becomes, emotionally and sometimes relationally.

Being *triumphant in the trenches* means never giving up, staying true to who you are, and giving it your best every single day. I read that Walt Disney filed for bankruptcy and came close to it several times before he finally succeeded in his endeavor to establish Disneyland. Many other millionaires have failed first before they were able to accomplish their goals. I have read, "Failure only occurs when you stop trying." We grow from the failures we experience in life, and as we admit our mistakes, they become the catalyst that catapults us into our destiny.

After the second year of being unemployed, my husband decided to pursue his Ph.D. using the Post-9/11 GI Bill. The benefits exceeded our expectations. It was like the Montgomery GI Bill on steroids. It had been almost twenty years since my husband had completed his MBA at Babson College, in Massachusetts, and he was excited about going back to school. Under this benefit, the military paid for his education or would allow him to transfer it to one of our unmarried children. If he didn't use the benefit promptly, he would lose it. Thus, he matriculated into Alliant International University in San Diego in 2011. This undertaking proved invaluable, and I believe it gave him the drive and momentum to stay positive while waiting on the answer concerning employment. I always encouraged those going through the Transition Readiness Seminar (TRS) to have a plan B—maybe even a plan C and D.

triumphant in the trenches means never giving up, staying true to who you are, and giving it your best every single day.

We were working hard to keep our home life steady and making sure the bills were paid as our youngest daughter began to pursue her career in the music industry. Like most who pursue this endeavor, it was a crazy whirlwind experience over the next six years. Rearing gifted and driven children can have a tremendous impact on your time, not to mention your finances and other resources. We wanted to support their dreams and help them get wherever they were trying to aspire in their careers. Even when it put a strain on us, we had a choice, and we did what we felt was best at the time.

Countless hours were spent on the highways all over Southern California, chauffeuring our youngest daughter to performances and competitions, from the Southern California Miss Junior Teen pageant to performing on *The X Factor* with a girl group. The investment has definitely played a huge part in her success as she continues to pursue her music career and establish her own entertainment company. Working in the entertainment industry presents its own set of issues, and dealing with numerous personalities was a challenge my daughter learned to manage quite well early on when she was introduced to sandpaper people. *When there was an obstacle, she stepped over it or on it to reach the next level.*

For the next six years, in my new position as a Transition Readiness Advisor, I dedicated my life to providing guidance, support, and career coaching in the areas of finance, resume writing, interviewing skills, and education. I worked alongside the Veterans Assistance team and the Department of Labor to help those transitioning out of the service. This opportunity allowed me to touch the lives of tens of thousands in that period, and I am so much the better for it.

With every session, I was exposed to the joys and tears of those faced with life-changing decisions. Some of them had no plan or direction. Some had no family to return to, and some were destitute because their life's dream was to have a full career in the military, but life happened, and they were now on a different course.

> When there was an obstacle, she stepped over it or on it to reach the next level.

Triumphant Thinking

1. Great sacrifices produce great rewards.
2. Understand the season you are in so that you can flourish where you are
3. Good follow ship prepares for great Leadership.

CHAPTER 19

The Next Game Plan

The many hours he spent under the tutelage of our pastor and working behind the scenes in the church gave my husband an up-close and personal look at servanthood at its finest. His over twenty-two years of serving our country were now coming into play on a different level. Within every organization, there are rewards and challenges. As the times change, people change, and we too must change to keep up with the economy and the diversity of people that we encounter. *It takes courage and stamina to continue to care about people when some don't care for themselves or you.* Not everyone is a team player, and not everyone exemplifies the same character as the leader.

We were raised in homes where both of our fathers were Pentecostal pastors, so serving was second nature to us. This trait was exemplified in our home as we reared our children. It was not an option whether to serve in some capacity within the community, with teams at school and in other extracurricular areas. We visited nursing homes to speak with those who had no one, and we sang, played instruments, and showed kindness. In some cases, our presence was enough. This is servanthood. Teaching the value of caring, appreciating where you are and what you have, and sharing it freely with others was the norm.

As my husband incorporated his class schedule into an already committed day, he poured even more into the life of our youngest daughter, as he now was the

> It takes courage and stamina to continue to care about people when some don't care for themselves or you.

chauffeur to and from school, to track meets, basketball games, girl group rehearsals, and any event she could squeeze into a day. This quality time was so impressionable upon her life that it yielded a powerful return in her future decisions and choices. I believe the decision to graduate from high school a year early and to apply, audition, and get accepted to the only university (University of Southern California) she applied for was driven partially by the investment my husband made during this period. I'm sure it influenced her character and outlook on life. Life had thrown us a curveball, but we adjusted and knocked it out of the park. This most influential time would have never happened had my husband found a job quickly.

Calling for Winners

Average was and is not an option! We instilled a spirit and attitude of excellence in our children, as well as other's children. We didn't allow them to think on a below-average level. One way we did this was by example. The other way was to ensure they were involved in numerous activities that exposed them to many facets of life. Our theory was that exposure and experience could do things we could not. It would also reinforce and complement our efforts.

We encouraged (okay...insisted) that they do their best in school, athletics, music, church activities, and practically everything they participated in. By modeling a strong spiritual foundation and providing a moral compass, we made it easier for them to mimic a winner's attitude. I must admit, we have great children, and they wanted to excel. We couldn't force them to find their greatness. We just provided an atmosphere that nurtured it.

Not only are military children resilient, but they are challenged to strive for the "extraordinary" to strengthen their resolve to meet the day-to-day combat that comes with being a teenager and trying to fit in even when they are different. They normally do not try to keep up with the latest unhealthy trends, gangs, or groupies.

A winner soars above adversity, opposition, depression, and rejection. From the outset of the conflict, a winner assesses his or her opponent, strategizes his movements, finalizes the action plan, and then executes it. We told our children they were winners! They embraced that concept so much that they wrote a song called, "I'm a Winner." Their lives reflect what they believe. *Winning does not mean that you never fail, but it does mean you never lose.*

Our faith provided us with a plan for success and roadmap to seamlessly aid in navigating over, around, or through the roadblocks set in place by the enemy. These could be spiritual or natural. It depended on the circumstances at the time. As winners, we are equipped to stand against damaging emotions, such as depression, self-degradation, and self-pity. This is why it was so important to establish our family mission statement early on and to create our family values as we did. We repeated it and posted it in our home so that it became embedded in our children. We did this so they would fight the urge to give in to negative thinking or succumb to peer pressure or feeling they had not met our expectations as parents.

I believe every level you rise to in life is a success. Each success means "I've beaten the odds that said I wouldn't or couldn't." I had to keep moving no matter what distractions or disappointments came my way." It's the endgame that actually matters.

> Winning does not mean that you never fail, but it does mean you never lose.

A Family Mission Statement

Why did we establish a family mission statement, and what does that actually look like? Now that our children were older and entering their individual positions in life, they would face peer pressure and the harsh reality that not everyone had a caring home with parents who were both active in their lives. Not every child had what we were providing: a safe, happy home life. Some children are even angry, disappointed, broken, and abandoned. More than ever, we as parents had to make a firm declaration, because we realized we would have a lasting impact on our children during their teen years and as they were approaching young adulthood. They would be making serious choices based on what they had witnessed and been exposed to.

My husband created our "family core values," typed them up, framed them, and hung them on the wall in the stairwell of our home so each time we used the stairs, we would see them as a constant reminder.

Butler Family "Core Values"

God first
Love each other
Integrity
Loyalty
Trust God and each other
Cooperation
Positive attitude

In Stephen Covey's book *The 7 Habits of Highly Effective Families*, he provides great nuggets to help build strong family relationships and guidance on how to implement them.

There is no victory in the status quo.

For our family, the second habit plays a huge part in our lives and how to stay focused on who we want to be and the values and principles that govern our lives. The Covey habit, "Beginning with the end in mind," helped us to create a family mission/values statement. It took some time and many rewrites to get there. Yours will also evolve as your family grows and moves toward what you have established as a foundation. Key components such as forgiveness, compassion, and "charitability" take precedence. The next few years were very important and life changing for all of us.

There is no victory in the status quo. A winner is always moving forward to establish momentum, and the result is winning. As parents, we have been given the responsibility to raise good citizens and compassionate individuals who will make an impact on the world for the better. We have tried to provide opportunities for our children to do more than we were able to do and to excel in helping to make this a better world to live in. It requires endless hard work, but that is okay, because it is what keeps us moving forward. Remember, we are a military family, and my husband gave over twenty-two years of his life supporting our country. He was willing to sacrifice his life if it came to that. How much more should that same commitment or greater be extended to our family and our children who will carry on our legacy?

Triumphant Thinking

1. When the tables turn and are not in your favor, chart your own course.
2. Live free from mental bondage. Don't allow failures and disappointments to paralyze you. Your mental strength determines how you will rise above your circumstances.
3. Establish strong family values; they are the foundation for positive growth and will impact one's future.

CHAPTER 20

Delayed but Not Denied

While I was waiting for something great to happen, I had to stay productive. I occupied my mind and kept my hands busy doing constructive things that helped propel me forward. My husband stayed diligent to the cause of continual spiritual growth within our faith and worked alongside our pastor to uphold his vision and to build others while in the middle of his own trench.

After submitting more than three hundred job applications and going on only four interviews, he decided to widen his search and apply for positions worldwide. He said he needed to "widen his aperture." Never really thinking of it as a real possibility, but doing it out of due diligence, he pressed the send button one day, and life as we knew it changed. Within forty-five days, he was on his way to the Kingdom of Saudi Arabia. Just when we had hit a smooth stride in our relationship, we were faced with yet another big challenge that lingered for a long time.

> Time is the agent of prosperity and growth if you allow it.

We honestly did not know what to expect, but we trusted that this was the divine plan for his life and believed that it was the answer to our prayers. Did we have any reservations, concerns, maybe even some fears? Of course, but because of our strong faith, we believed we had been given a sound mind and the power to overcome any fear. We reflected on previous tough situations, and the answers that always prevailed were in our favor. Surprisingly, there are thousands of retirees working overseas. *Time is the agent of prosperity and growth if you allow it.*

What would I do now? Our youngest daughter was a few weeks from graduating from high school and attending the University of Southern California (USC) Thornton Music Performance program. She said this was the only school she wanted to attend, and it was the only one she applied for. The odds of getting into any highly reputable university were slim, and the process would be arduous. We encouraged her to apply to others, but she was vision-minded and committed to her dream. If you can believe it, you can achieve it!

Talk about a lesson learned from a seventeen-year-old. This was my first time having to follow through with all things related to admissions—housing, the move, finances, etc. Because my faithful, dependable, organized husband, the king of college admissions and all things

Life will often present the opportunity for us to meet the person face to face, who we have had inside of us all along.

related, was now over 7,500 miles away from me, I had to face this new challenge on my own. I really didn't have time to think about how I felt at the moment. I knew it had to be done. Deadlines were approaching and had to be met. I hadn't realized how strong and capable I really was until I had to complete these tasks on my own.

I hadn't recognized how comfortable I had become since my husband handled most of the academic ventures concerning our children. I realized I had allowed somewhat of a complacent spirit to creep in on me when it came to certain academic tasks. Maybe because I had put my advanced degree optimism to sleep in order to support the dreams of my family. Stepping up to assist my youngest daughter sparked that interest again and maybe in the future, I'll revisit it.

So a new chapter began for all of us. *Life will often present the opportunity for us to meet the person face to face, who we have had inside of us all along.*

Relocating to a new country, with a foreign culture, workforce, expectations, and environment was not easy and was very stressful. The assignment was given at one of the most critical times in my husband's life. Retired from the military, we were looking forward to a life of family time and creating memories that had been put on hold for over twenty-two years. Life was now interrupted. From my standpoint, it seemed intentional.

Why couldn't he have found a job here in California or even in the United States? Why across the world, thousands of miles away? Yes, I asked these questions and struggled with it after he was gone. It happened so fast, I really didn't have time to digest it while it was actually happening. I asked myself later, "Did I agree to this?" I knew that I had, just as I had always supported my husband in doing what he thought best for our family.

I regrouped, prayed, and stood up to meet the challenge. I believe I have found my greatest strength amid the greatest adversity. This was part of the process of becoming who I was created to be, and as I discovered, if I just allowed the process to work, I would become a masterpiece.

When greatness is a part of your destiny and you are in a place where you may be feeling like you are suffocating or not fully using your potential, a door may open to place you right where you need to be just so that everything can happen. That's not to say you can't answer the call right where you are with diligence and steadfastness, but if you have tried and it seems you have hit a brick wall, it makes sense to do something about it. Someone said, "Insanity is doing the same thing and expecting to get a different result."

When my husband retired, I thought our days of being geographically separated were over, but we found ourselves learning to live as a couple on two separate continents literally half way around the world for over five years. How would this work? Although we were familiar with temporary separations and deployments that had worked out in the past, this was not the plan for our empty-nest years. Now the nest was empty for real, and we were both alone. Didn't see this trench coming.

This is not an ideal situation I would recommend to any couple, no matter how long you have been married. We had been together at that time for over thirty years and had worked hard at enjoying a complete, fulfilling, and wonderful marriage, and now it would be tested with an extended period of distance. We were both now experiencing life changes that come along with getting older. You depend on each other in different ways, and now, here we are, geographically separated. As in any marriage, from newlyweds to those who have had the wonderful blessing of being married for sixty years or more, time together was precious and had become more important than ever.

I was working at a military installation, advising military couples and individuals about their transition into the civilian sector. I educated them on scenarios that might occur based on the choices they made for their future and spoke candidly of the pitfalls and challenges they would face. The reality was that the ideal opportunity might not come immediately, and the strength of their relationship would be tested. It would take constant and effective communication to enjoy a successful transition.

Staying focused on helping others helped me keep my sanity as the months apart turned to years—three, then four, then five. We would make sure to rendezvous in wonderful places every three or four months to reconnect and revisit this plan, making sure we could handle it. Otherwise, we would abandon it and move in another direction.

I applaud military spouses who have survived the years of struggle, separation, and mental stress. They are worthy of their own Medal of Honor. Each time I have encountered a military spouse, I have walked away feeling honored and humbled. These special individuals are valiant, compassionate, and wise. They are the primary reason I am writing my memoirs and sharing how to be *triumphant in the trenches*.

Triumphant Thinking

1. Remain flexible so unexpected changes do not destroy you.
2. Prepare for your upgrade. Better lifestyle, relationships and your health.
3. If you don't plan for your future, your future plans may fail.

CHAPTER 21

Sacrifice—That's What We Do

Year after year, we revisited our plan and looked at the time we had already spent apart. Many people, although well-intentioned, would ask, "Why are you still living here in the States and not there with your husband?" These inquiries became more frequent when I began to deal with my health challenges. Two carpal tunnel surgeries and deteriorating knees added to the concerns of others, who felt I should be with my husband while facing these situations. *Sometimes, sacrifice weighs the heaviest when the ideal circumstance isn't attainable at the time.*

I appreciated the concern from many family members and friends, but I could not abandon the assignments that had been placed in my hands. Right or wrong, I was created with purpose, and my husband and I agreed it was time to pursue my goals and not neglect what I was called to do. Our marriage has grown tremendously during this time of challenge. The reality of us as two wholes joined to make one really doesn't make sense from a biological common sense perspective, but it is absolutely the truth. We are joined in a covenant relationship, bringing a total person with gifts, talents, flaws, and space to grow in unity with another, and therefore, we are greater and stronger together—especially when we move in agreement.

Our individual mission to be better, more loving, and more compassionate to each other grew greater with each passing year. This could only happen because we are both complete as individuals. We

> Sometimes, sacrifice weighs the heaviest when the ideal circumstance isn't attainable at the time.

have lived our lives to *include* each other, yet *not totally dependent* on each other. This was a fundamental principle for coping with long geographical separations and accepting each other's different passions, hobbies, and career choices.

I was determined to live as an example, especially for my children—that love, in its purest form, can survive anything. Society has promoted what is glamorous and unrealistic as truth, thereby giving our upcoming generations a false sense of success, love, and acceptance.

Achieving a healthy and happy marriage takes work, and you must put in the time to win. I am committed to speaking a life of truth through example within my own personal relationships and to teach our children that they are special individuals and must manifest their own greatness without the boundaries set by others, especially with regards to what others think.

Our marriage has not gone without tests, but it has always weathered the storms, and with grace and mercy. Because of our desire to please God and the fact that we held each other accountable to a high biblical standard, we are victorious. This truly helped us build a strong, loving, and compassionate relationship with each other and our children. Our healthy relationship has helped our children become healthy and balanced individuals. This high standard defines the character of each person and provides restraints that we would not impose on ourselves without faith as a driving factor.

The big reality sat in as I watched my children grow into young adults. They are actually great people and listened to their dad and me after all—at least, for the most part. It was my time to start shifting, to let go and watch them spread their wings.

I don't know how this shift affects other parents (and mothers in particular), but it has definitely proved to be one of the most difficult tasks of my life. How do you go from being the nurturer, confidant, problem-solver, encourager, and rescuer to just Mom? I had to realize that I was still all of the above, but only filling those roles as needed, not at my discretion. I learned that to enable children to soar, you must allow them to hit their own walls and stub their own toes as part of their journey. I also realized they could not do so at my expense. I'll talk more about that in my next book.

Accepting the shift in our lives has been monumental. My own personal endeavors allowed me to enjoy a career as a certified career coach, public speaker, workshop facilitator, life coach, and advisor. The rewards of making a difference in the lives of others were a sense of accomplishment and fulfillment. Leaving this routine and comfortable place of familiarity was quite an emotional journey.

I began transitioning my thoughts to arrive at this place with clarity and assurance that it was the right time. After at least six months of redirecting my focus, I now had to determine how I would find my place in the next season of my life. Each time we relocated to a new city, we had to adapt to a new neighborhood, new schools, a new church, new organizations, even redefine our identity within the workforce or volunteer organizations. The severity of the impact depended on where we were and what was available to us.

Every time I had to find my connection all over again, I experienced stress, uncertainty, the possibility of rejection, and sometimes concerns for safety. One of the most reassuring things we depended on was the knowledge we could connect with complete strangers within the military community and feel welcomed because they had experienced very similar transitions and challenging adjustments. This time, it would not only be another city, but another country and a radically different culture. It's all about timing and being open to what your destiny is exposing you to. The lives I have been assigned to touch and impact were waiting for me.

So here I was, finding myself in a similar situation as the many military members I had been advising for years. I had helped them prepare for their new journeys and ask the difficult questions. I did not think this is what I would be doing when I retired. It was time to reevaluate my own goals and put a plan of action in motion. I now had to take my own advice.

I thought I knew what I would do when I retired. The plan was to relax, declutter my house from all of the buildup from over thirty-five years of world travel, and remove all the keepsakes from my children, who were now young adults and living on their own. I wasn't getting rid of the memories and experiences, but downsizing the excess. When I actually had a few days to walk around and look at some of the things

I had accumulated, I realized it was just stuff. I needed to offload it and prepare for the shift into the next season of my life.

Creating a schedule to plan out the next stage of my life helped me declutter. I found that the clutter in our lives can mirror our emotional state of being. The reason we can only take a certain number of suitcases per person on the airplane is to make sure there is sufficient storage space for everyone's luggage. Also, how fast you can travel in the sky is based on several components, and weight is a key player. *If you are going to be triumphant in the trenches, you must get rid of the excess that can slow you down or cause you to drop or lose altitude.* My decision to live above the newly created circumstances catapulted me into a fruitful, prosperous, and healthy future.

My life as a military spouse was and still is phenomenal. The shift from active-duty to retired-veteran spouse has proven to be the most enlightening, rewarding, and adventurous season I could have ever asked for. Conversations, emotions, locations, friendships, struggles, forgiveness, victories, disappointments, setbacks, recognitions, rejections, sacrifices, joys, tears, growing pains, elation, stamina, adjustments, love, health challenges, peace, promises, deceit, uncertainty, and faith are all a part of the memories that have brought me to this place in time. I will be forever grateful for the life that I have been given, knowing I am just beginning to write my next chapter of life by completing this one.

Now, here I am, sitting at a kitchen table in the Saudi Arabia, looking back over my life and the divinely strategic experiences that have occurred. I use the word strategic (meaning, "carefully designed or planned to serve a particular purpose or advantage") to express the importance of why I wrote my memoirs. Not only is this a historical recap of my life from my perspective but also a guide with valuable nuggets of wisdom, years of experience, and tried-and-true methods for living *triumphantly in the trenches.*

I wrote my story hoping to give hope to someone on his or her own journey— whether in the beginning, the middle, or even toward the end. Regardless of where

> If you are going to be triumphant in the trenches, you must get rid of the excess that can slow you down or cause you to drop or lose altitude.

you are, I hope at least one experience I have shared will help you live victoriously and operate in the most positive and productive space in your mind. My memoir was intended to leave a legacy for my family and encourage spouses everywhere that they too can overcome and be trendsetters for future generations, who I pray will positively affect the world and live *triumphantly in the trenches.*

Triumphant Thinking

1. Release the weights of your past so that you can enjoy the freedom in your future.
2. Stay committed to your goals and focused on your dreams as you navigate the twists and turns of life.
3. Emotions can take us to places we don't want to go, but self-control can manage to assist us so that we grow as we go.

CONCLUSION

While I was finishing the last chapter of this book, death and grief unexpectedly struck again. I experienced another trench of life. During a recent trip home to Oklahoma to celebrate my husband's fortieth high school reunion, we stopped in Oklahoma City on our way to Lawton, Oklahoma, my husband's hometown. We enjoyed a wonderful evening of fellowship with my brother, his wife, and my nieces and nephew. Less than twenty-four hours later, I received a phone call from my brother wife's, who said, "We lost Jim."

I asked, very emotionally, "Jim who," because I just knew she wasn't referring to my brother. I was wrong. Seemingly out of nowhere, my brother died of a massive heart attack.

Words cannot express the loss and devastation this brought to my family and me. Yet, in the midst of this, I am forever grateful for the opportunity I could fly in the day before, break bread, and hug his neck one more time. I consider this a gift from God. He loved me enough to give me that time with my brother.

My brother was a man of great integrity, purpose, commitment, and drive. He was charismatic, highly intelligent, prophetic, gifted in many ways, in good health and mental resolve. Nevertheless, he took leave from the cares of this world and received his crown of glory.

I have written several times throughout my memoir about the devastation of loss and grief and disappointment. I am still convinced that you can be *triumphant in the trenches* while dealing with the tragedies and pain that comes with life. We realize life ultimately comes to an end, and we all must prepare for that inevitable point in time. I encourage each of you to take the time to appreciate and enjoy moments with your family. Take time to plan events and just slow down. We only pass through this life one time, so don't waste it.

BIG! BIG! BIG!

Wow, where do we go from here? The final chapter hasn't been written. I know that the next chapters will be BIG! BIG! BIG! The promise of greater things to come is already here. Living my best and blessed life is more than a cliché. Every story, experience, person, and situation that has been a part of my life has shaped me for this journey. I live with great anticipation for the next step. *As optimistic as I am—trust me—I am quite aware that I cannot control or precisely predict the future, but I can control how I experience it.* The gifts and resources that have been placed in my hands are priceless, and I can be trusted with them.

I believe I have experienced only a small portion of what is to come and that it is limitless, because I see it before I can see it. I have visualized where I am going and have spoken it out of my mouth to give it credence, and now I will step into it with boldness.

As I move into the next adventure of my life, I hope to unfold the many proverbs of life that have been my mainstays and escorted me to this point in time.

When service members have gone through all of the proper training, the physical preparation, the mental and emotional challenges, and when they are deemed ready for service, they can accomplish what they were prepared for—but only if they are confident and believe deep down inside that they are ready. The next step is their assignment. They just do it!

Being *triumphant in the trenches* depends on what you *believe* you can be. Your background, lack of money, lack of solid family support, and lack of education are excuses for inaction. Everything you need to succeed is already inside. It takes a made-up mind and a conscious decision to change your path. I sought out the resources and people that were doing what I wanted to do and

> I am quite aware that I cannot control or precisely predict the future, but I can control how I experience it.

learned how they did it. I had to gird up my thought processes and become relentless in the pursuit of my goals. During this pursuit, I learned to be always kind, considerate, and professional. There will be deterrents, distractions, derailments, dislocations, and even disappointments along the way, but I know that each one also brings growth, strength, renewed commitment, reward, and success.

Rise up, make a decision, activate your faith, and implement your plan with an "I can" attitude, or just do something you desire. I encourage you to take the step. Jump into the trenches of life, and begin living triumphantly!

Triumphant Thinking

1. Living a life of abundance is within your reach, just go for it.
2. The future—it hasn't happened yet, but what you do in the present will dictate it.
3. Trenches may always be in your path, just prepare to rise out of them triumphantly.
4. Live life to the fullest. It's been said, Leave empty don't die full.

TRIUMPHANT THINKING

(Nuggets of Wisdom)

1. Great relationships are the result of the investment. Plan to commit your time and energy for the long haul.
2. Revisit expectations often, they change just as you will.
3. Learn the art of effective communication and use it.
4. You need to know what you're getting yourself into before you marry, there will be an adjustment phase. Seek counsel or guidance before and after marriage.
5. Discuss your family principles and values to gain a better understanding of who he or she is.
6. Realize that your validation does not come only from your spouse. You must know who you are and the value you bring to the relationship.
7. Invest in yourself. Read books and information that will educate and equip you to adapt to the culture of a new lifestyle. This principle applies to anyone embarking upon a career that takes you into the political arena, or one that delves into the world of a Fortune 500 company. You must be aware and astute to stroll graciously and fit into your new lifestyle with confidence and knowledge.
8. Find a mentor. Be aware of those seasoned individuals you may be able to tap into. Don't be afraid to ask for help and guidance.

9. Build upon every disappointment and turn it into a victory.
10. Allow your inner warrior to rise in times of despair and setbacks.
11. You are stronger than you think, and sometimes you have to prove it to yourself.
12. Allow challenge to strengthen your resolve. The outcome is a testament to who you are and the caliber of your character.
13. The sandpaper people are placed in your life intentionally. Allow the process to refine you.
14. Keep communication open with your children as you experience change together.
15. Allow challenge to strengthen your resolve. The outcome is a testament to who you are and the caliber of your character.
16. The sandpaper people are placed in your life intentionally. Allow the process to refine you.
17. Keep communication open with your children as you experience change together.
18. A setback is really just a setup for an upcoming victory in your life.
19. Don't get too hung up on yourself. Focus on helping others.
20. Trenches and opportunity show you who you really are. They build character.
21. No matter how difficult your life is, someone else is worse off.
22. Connecting with a support group is essential.
23. Challenge promotes growth if you can handle it.
24. 3. Stay the course. It's what you attain at the end that brings the most joy.
25. Get a new "mind-itude." Change how you think about your circumstances. What you visualize is what you bring into existence.
26. Appreciate the people who are strategically placed in your life. You may not know why initially, but it is on purpose.
27. Faith is an agent in assisting us to get through some of the toughest times we must face. Grow strong in yours daily. You'll never know when you will need it most.
28. When encountering grief, whether it is the loss of a loved one or a shift in your life's status, allow it to take its natural course over time. Seek help, if needed.

29. We all experience loss at some time. Knowing where to go for help will assist you in getting you through it (e.g., the stages of grief and counseling).
30. When your plans seem to fail, you redirect, because that was not the direction you were meant to go in anyway.
31. Never allow the fears or ignorance displayed by someone else to detour you from your destiny.
32. Believe that wherever you go, someone will be there to affect your life positively.
33. Adversity will bring out the best or the worst in you.
34. Make lemonade out of lemons. You may not find a job or start a career when you want to, but you have everything necessary to be successful inside of you.
35. Transparency brings liberation. Be true to yourself and acknowledge when you are not soaring with the eagles but are temporarily flying low. It's okay, and you will be okay.
36. Make memories with your family and focus on the good times while you have them. It's really all that counts.
37. Selflessness brings unexpected rewards.
38. What looks like it was designed to break you was designed to build you.
39. Say yes to new doors that may open even when you're not sure why you should walk through them.
40. It's your choice how you handle what happens to you. Always go high.
41. Criticism is actually a prop to take you to the next level. Use it and keep it moving.
42. Life has a tendency to course correct; accept it, it is working for your good.
43. Establish strong principles early to maintain strong character later.
44. Be your authentic self. Don't confuse who you want to be with who you are.
45. Allow your natural gifts and talents to position you for your next level assignment.
46. Have a solid exit plan for retirement, or you may have to come out of it later.

47. Learn the strengths of your children's personalities so you can live more harmoniously.
48. Some parenting methods may seem harsh to your children at the time, but no concern at all would be unproductive in the end.
49. Proper positioning prepares for opportunity.
50. Preparation positions you for success.
51. Taking action accesses the open door.
52. Great sacrifices produce great rewards.
53. Understand the season you are in so that you can flourish where you are
54. Good follow ship prepares for great Leadership.
55. When the tables turn and are not in your favor, chart your own course.
56. Live free from mental bondage. Don't allow failures and disappointments to paralyze you. Your mental strength determines how you will rise above your circumstances.
57. Establish strong family values; they are the foundation for positive growth and will impact one's future.
58. Remain flexible so unexpected changes do not destroy you.
59. Prepare for your upgrade. Better lifestyle, relationships and your health.
60. If you don't plan for your future, your future plans may fail.
61. Release the weights of your past so that you can enjoy the freedom in your future.
62. Stay committed to your goals and focused on your dreams as you navigate the twists and turns of life.
63. Emotions can take us to places we don't want to go, but self-control can manage to assist us so that we grow as we go.
64. Living a life of abundance is within your reach, just go for it.
65. The future—it hasn't happened yet, but what you do in the present will dictate it.
66. Trenches may always be in your path, just prepare to rise out of them triumphantly.
67. Live life to the fullest. It's been said, leave empty don't die full.

REFERENCES

1. Five Stages of Grief by Kubler Ross https://www.psycom.net/depression.central.grief.html
2. The Five Love Languages by Dr. Gary Chapman
3. Seven Habits of Highly Effective People by Steven Covey
4. The Seven Stages of the Emotional Cycle of Deployment by Marine Corps Family Team Building
5. Militaryonesource.com

Resources

1. Book: A Family's Guide to the Military for Dummies
2. Book: Basics from the Barracks
3. Book: Military Etiquette and Protocol
4. Book: A spouse's quick reference to its unique customs, courtesies, and tradition
5. Encouragement for America's Hidden Heroes Survival tactics for the families of our military forces.
6. Militarymentors.com

ABOUT THE AUTHOR

Kathryn A. Butler is an Author, Certified Master Trainer Instructor, and Certified Career Coach. She has also been a highly sought after speaker for conferences both nationally and internationally for over 30 years.

Her selflessness, big heart, and effervescent personality are always on full throttle. She gracefully navigated the storms associated with fourteen permanent change of station (PCS) moves over the course of twenty-two years of being a military spouse, and dealt with constant uncertainty with style and grace. Kathryn has been happily married to her husband, Dr. Preston Butler Jr. (retired US Army lieutenant colonel), for 37 years.

Kathryn and Preston were blessed with three beautiful military "brats" who all received their advanced degrees at universities in California.

Kathryn inspires, validates, and motivates all whom she encounters. Her "triumphant thinking" nuggets provide sage wisdom in how to maneuver successfully through life at any stage.

Contact Information

Kathryn A. Butler
kathrynabutler1@gmail.com
Personal & Professional Development
Certifications: CCC, CEIP, and CWDP

AUTHOR'S NOTE

My time as a military spouse was so impactful that I feel as though I earned a degree in "military life." I am thankful for the years I spent traveling around the world with my family as my husband's career blossomed. I wish to pay sincere tribute to the military services, military service members, and military dependents. Each group contributes in its own special way to our great nation. I share my memoirs in this book to inform, inspire, and encourage spouses (as well as the entire military family). The ultimate goal is to show you that regardless of the struggles, you can be *triumphant in the trenches*.